Poetry in the Caribbean

Julie Pearn

Introduction by Louise Bennett

HODDER AND STOUGHTON

LONDON SYDNEY AUCKLAND TORONTO

Contents

Introduction		iii
Chapter 1	What is poetry?	1
Chapter 2	Talking about poetry	5
Chapter 3	Whose voice, whose version? Caribbean poetry and the achievement of nationhood	8
Chapter 4	The people's language	16
Chapter 5	Brathwaite and Walcott — poets national and international	21
Chapter 6	Poems of protest	29
Chapter 7	Roots and other routes	36
Chapter 8	Emergent voices	43
Chapter 9	Why is poetry important?	51
Glossary		54
Further Reading and Listening		58

British Library Cataloguing in Publication Data

Pearn, Julie
Poetry in the Caribbean.
1. West Indian poetry (English)—History and criticism
I. Title
811   PR9212

ISBN 0 340 36005 4

First published 1985
Copyright © 1985 by Julie Pearn

All rights reserved. No part of this publication may be reproduced or transmitted in any form or by any means, elestronic or mechanical, including photocopy, recording, or any information storage or retrieval system, without permission in writing from the publisher.

Printed in Great Britain for Hodder and Stoughton Educational, a division of Hodder and Stoughton Ltd, Mill Road, Dunton Green, Sevenoaks, Kent, by St Edmundsbury Press, Bury St Edmunds, Suffolk.

Acknowledgments

This book could not have been written without the advice, encouragement and inspiration of these people, and many more: E. K. Brathwaite, Mervyn Morris, Andrew Salkey, John La Rose, Miss Lou, Christiane Keane, Anson Gonzalez, Abdul Malik, Stewart Brown, Gordon Rohlehr, Anne Walmsley. Grateful thanks to all.

The author and publishers are grateful to the following for permission to reproduce illustrations in this book:

Jonathan Cape Ltd (photographer: Rollie McKenna) (page 21); Dave Saunders (pages 1 and 5); Haroldo Palo Jr/NHPA (page 6); Commonwealth Institute (page 2); Kraus-Thomson Organization Ltd/Caribbean Quarterly (page 3); Victoria and Albert Museum (page 9); BBC Hulton Picture Library (pages 9, 14 and 23); Bim (page 11); Barbados Board of Tourism/Infopress Limited (page 13); The British Library (pages 16 and 44); National Library of Jamaica (pages 17, 18, 22, 29, 39); Bruce St. John (page 19); RT Studios (page 22); Philip Wolmuth (pages 24, 34, 43, 46 and 52); Zomo Publicity (page 24); Jamaica Information Service (photographer: Errol Harvey) (page 26); Jamaica Information Service (photographer: Dennis Richardson) (pages 36 and 51); John and Penny Hubley (pages 30 and 49); Thomas Nelson and Son Ltd. (page 31); Julian Stapleton (pages 32, 33 and 40); Dennis Scott (page 37); Lorna Goodison (pages 38 and 47); Randolph Alleyne (page 41); Sangster's Bookstores (page 45); Anne Cardale (page 53); Anthony McNeill (page 39). The author and publishers would also like to thank the following for permission to use photographs on the front cover: Julian Stapleton (top left); London Weekend Television/Commonwealth Institute (bottom left); Faber & Faber (top right); Mark Lumley (bottom right).

Introduction

In the very first chapter of *Poetry in the Caribbean* Julie Pearn writes: 'We find poetry all around us. It does not only exist in books.' These words warmed my heart to the manuscript.

When I was a child, each day contained a poem of folk songs, folk stories, street cries, legends, proverbs, riddles, tales of Moonshine darlin' or Ring Ding, ni-nights (ninth night), Dinkey Miny, Duppy stories, Rolling calf, Whooping boy and oh, I was fascinated by the drums at nights coming from the hills, the Pokomina drums, Kumina drums, Burro drums. At Christmas time I loved to watch the John Cunno dancers and listen to the tales about the different characters in the masquerade, how Koo-Koo who dances with a house on his head is really the symbol of our strength (him lickle but him tallawah – he is small but very strong). How Ass Head is the clown of the masquerade (jus' a play fool fe ketch wise – pretending to be stupid to gain knowledge). All the things in our oral tradition, handed down to us from generation to generation, were very much alive and vibrant around and about me. I was excited by them though I sensed that they were not considered respectable. They had no social status. They were not the things to which one should aspire, not the things that one should desire to learn about or indulge in. In fact, they were to be deplored and despised as coming from the offspring of slaves who were illiterate, uncultured and downright stupid. We were taught and encouraged to sing the songs of foreign countries, to learn foreign folk dances and stories as these foreign things were considered infinitely better than things West Indian. The general and accepted trend was to be as European as possible.

But though we did not sing our folk songs in school, we would sing them to each other in the school-yard at recess time. We would recall the digging songs we heard on the way to school when we passed the street-repair workers digging up the street and singing to the rhythm of the pick axes. We would swap stories about Anancy, the 'trickify' little spider man who speaks with a lisp and lives by his wits. He is both comic and sinister, both hero and villain of the folk stories. Bra'nancy, as he is affectionately called, is a lovable rascal who has magical powers and his stories make it quite plain that he is able to get away with tricks which ordinary mortals can't. Every existing custom is said to have been started by Anancy (is Anancy meck it).

We enjoyed the tales of Ribba Mumma, the fish woman who lives in the deepest hole in the river and comes up every soon-a-mawnin (early morning) to comb her hair with a golden comb made for her by the river, and to sing her special little song, 'dah me dah Ribba Mumma'.

Then some child who used to live in the country parts would tell of Dinky Miny where we banish grief, 'teck kin teet kibba heart bun' (use laughter to cover sorrow). Dinky is held every night night for eight nights after a death to cheer up the family of the dead and prevent them from grieving. Nothing sad must happen at a Dinky. People sing their loudest, laugh their loudest and dance with exaggerated abandon at the Dinky.

We would recall tales of Moonshine Darlin' or Ring Ding on moonshine nights when people of all age groups would gather in a yard or just underneath a large tree to sing tunes, play ring games and tell stories and riddles as long as the moon lasted.

Song: Moonshine tonight, come meck we
        dance an sing

> Me dah rock so, you dah rock so
> Under Banyan tree.

We would swap riddles: 'Riggle me dis, riggle me dat, guess me dis riggle and perhaps not.' 'One piece a yellow yam serve de whole worl' — moon. 'Longulong, longulong, nutten no long like longulong' — road.

We found that all of us shared a common love for the folklore, things that were so much an indigenous part of our country and our people. We did not know the word indigenous, but somehow we could feel it.

There is a folk proverb common to the Caribbean which says, 'When drum beat goat skin tremble, when horn blow cow head shake.' We respond to the things that are a part of us (most drum heads are covered with goat skin, cow horns are used to make music). As I grew older I became convinced that our folklore was not born out of stupidity and ignorance but out of the creative and artistic abilities of our people. Ours is a rich heritage of artistic expression which contains much of beauty, grace, strength, dignity and the secrets of survival. I was convinced that the language of the people, the folk speech which many condemned as bad talking, was good. Most of the people I knew and loved, people who were kind and good, talked in this language. The majority of our people spoke it, all of our people understood it and it was the most natural and vital means of expression in the country. Because it is rich in wit and humour, there are those who would dismiss the folk speech lightly as a language of laughter and tend to ignore the fact that this is the first language for a vast number of our people. They have lived and loved and suffered and rejoiced in the language for centuries, talking nothing else. Those people have left us a rich heritage of oral literature and creative expressions in songs, stories, legends, proverbs, and vibrant music of which we can be proud.

The movement towards political independence in the Caribbean inspired our creative artists, painters, writers, musicians to a new cultural expression with a dominant Caribbean flavour.

Our poetry is now reflecting the realities of our life, creating our heroes, and heroines, speaking our own language, presenting the authentic tragedy, drama and comedy of our own life-style and portraying our own unique way of life. Caribbean writing now has gained the momentum and vitality of the Caribbean people with a strong focus on the 'folk element'. The wealth of traditional customs and rituals, which are a direct expression of our African heritage, form a vital, strong and unending source for our written literature. Though Asian and European cultures have had much influence on our cultural development, the African traditions remain the strongest element and the dominant feature.

> For wen de Asian Culture,
> An de European Culture,
> Buck up pon African Culture
> In de Caribbean People . . .

> We stir dem up an blen' dem to we flavour!
> We shake dem up an move dem to we beat!
> We weel dem an we tun dem,
> An we rock dem an we soun' dem,
> An we tempo dem,
> An lawks de rydim sweet!
> An de beat . . .
> Is de Caribbean rydim!

This rhythm now moves with authority through both the oral and written literature of the Caribbean people.

Louise Bennett-Coverley
January 1985

1 What is poetry?

Does a poem have to *rhyme*? Must it have a special *rhythm*? All of us have probably heard or read poems which do not rhyme, so that cannot be a hard and fast rule. Are there any rules at all? Nowadays, **calypsoes** and the *lyrics* of Bob Marley's songs are widely accepted as poetry. In fact, once the barriers are down, we might as well accept all song lyrics, rhymes on Christmas cards, and advertising jingles as poems of a kind.

At least we can recognise the 'family' we are talking about. It does not mean to say we cannot exercise our judgement. Obviously some poems are far more rewarding than others, and it is good to be able to select those which are and to say why.

What we do see if we look at this poetry 'family' in a very broad way are patterns of words being put together in quite an artificial fashion, if we compare them with everyday speech. For example, most song lyrics are shaped every few words by a rhyme, which is hardly very natural. And yet poetry, this artificial form, has an ancient place in human culture, and plays an important part, whether sung, spoken or printed, in every society in the world.

What we are doing, whether we are staging a calypso contest or a very quiet and serious poetry reading, is creating a situation in which words are given a special focus. We hear the artist manipulate words in a manner which is far from everyday use, but we accept and enjoy it,

Bob Marley and the I-Threes. The words of *Redemption Song, No Woman, No Cry, Get Up Stand Up* and many other Marley songs live on because they say so much about, and to, the Caribbean people. Marley was a musician, but he was also a poet.

because it creates special effects. We may be drawn in our imagination into the rhythmic motion of a train, or thrown into hysterical laughter by a witty play on words. We distinguish poetry from other uses of words by the degree of attention the poet gives to rhythm and shape in every word and *phrase*.

Although poetry involves a special use of language, it is also true that we find many features of poetry around us in everyday life. This is particularly so in the Caribbean, where there is a strong *oral tradition*.

If somebody boasts he is 'de man in demand', we may enjoy the phrase for itself, whether strictly true or not! He is actually making us aware of language in a poetic way as the sounds of 'de man' and 'demand' come out more or less the same. What we hear first is a pattern of sound. As we make sense of the pattern, we then appreciate its wit. The joker demonstrates that we can play with the sound and meaning of language.

One common quality of poetry is that it contains striking ways of expressing things. Poets often try to pack a good deal of meaning into a very few words. We all appreciate short, memorable phrases which say a lot. *Proverbs* are good examples. Many proverbs are like extremely short poems.

> De higher Monkey climb, de more he show he tail

This is a well-known proverb. It is memorable because it is funny, and because it brings to mind a vivid picture. We remember the exact words mainly through the way the proverb is balanced in two parts: 'De higher . . . de more . . .' This balance of two ideas is echoed in the rhythm. So the rhythm helps to reinforce our memory. Although we see the *literal* truth of the proverb, we know it is not just about monkeys, but about human beings, and that the kind of climbing being referred to is social climbing. We then work out the real and intended meaning of the proverb. We conclude that, just like monkeys, human beings' least beautiful aspects get exposed more and more as they gain a lofty position. The choice of a monkey as a comparison makes the ambitious person seem very ridiculous. In this proverb, we can see how a few words can be used to make a powerful statement. Because the idea is so well-expressed, we are strongly persuaded that it is true. These are just the same qualities the poet is aiming at.

Advertisers are well aware that rhythm helps to impress a phrase upon us. The slogan

> Things go better with Coca Cola
> Things go better with Coke

has been around for a long time. It is difficult at first to see why. It clearly does not mean very much. The empty words, however, lend themselves to a nice kind of **Salsa** beat. Whether we like it or not, we often find such phrases running through our head. Apart from the rhythm, though, this type of slogan is the poorest sort of poetry. Poetry aims to excite thought and imagination. This does the opposite.

Dan Maraya, Nigerian singer and musician, playing the Kuntigi. Poetry, whether sung, spoken or printed, plays a major part in every society.

Louise Bennett's *Back to Africa*, on the other hand, gives us an example of rhythm and sound being used for fun, but in a way which emphasises the meaning:

> What a debil of a bump-an-bore
> Rig-jig an palam-pam
> Ef de whole worl start fi go back
> Whe dem great grampa come from!

Here the words tumble over each other, giving through the sound the exact impression of chaos the poet is imagining.

There are other ways in which we can enjoy language for its sound value. Saying a tongue twister, for example. Repeating the same sound requires a lot of effort and practice. It can also make a special effect, as here, where the sound of the sea itself can be heard:

> She sells sea shells on the sea shore

Such effects, though we take them for granted, are poetic. We can certainly compare Derek Walcott's recreation of sea sounds:

> Behind us all the sky folded,
> as history folds over a fishline,
> and the foam foreclosed
> with nothing in our hands
> (*Names*)

The repeated 'f' sound echoes the sound of the sea foam as it fast disappears. The sound helps to bring the picture more vividly to mind. Through bringing to mind the disappearing quality of foam, Walcott also helps us to understand his view of history.

Lion, a calypsonian in Trinidad of the 1930s, used a technique of the **Midnight Robber**, a Carnival character, to emphasise how terrifying he is:

> Devastation, destruction, desolation and damnation
> All these I'll inflict on insubordination
> For the Lion in his power is like the Rock of Gibraltar.

Here we see words being carefully selected for effect. The repeated 'd's make a crashing sound, echoing the meaning, while all the long words ending in '-ation' add to an impression of Lion's invincibility. How can we challenge a man who is in command of so many long words?

A cartoon of the Midnight Cowboy.

A calypsonian can make power (pow-ah) rhyme with Gibraltar (Gibral-tah). Rhymes give words a very definite pattern and shape:

> Get up, stand up! Stand up for your rights.
> Get up, stand up! Don't give up the fight.
> (Bob Marley)

Rhymes are not a regular feature of modern spoken Caribbean poetry, but **dub** poets use them sometimes:

> earth a blaze
> man a rage
> man haffi live in a shanty
> food an clothes skanty
> (Oku Onuora, *A Slum Dweller Declares*)

We call words that sound very close, like 'blaze' and 'rage' half-rhymes.

Nearly all the poets use rhymes occasionally. The beachboys' leader Batto is 'the shake of their cake', in the words of Edward Kamau Brathwaite, while Eric Roach describes his mother 'Hoeing the growing'. Most modern poets use rhyme not as a rule, but for a particular effect.

One way of packing a lot of significance into a few words is to use double meaning. This is very popular with calypsonians, especially when they want to make innuendoes, and yet pretend to be innocent all the while. Bruce St. John uses a technique very close to the calypsonians in his poem *The Other Woman*. He is actually talking to his wife about the sea, but she can be forgiven for interpreting otherwise:

> If win' blow fore or aft
> She does go but she does come
> Go and come, she don' clear out
> A whole mont' straight like you does do
> *She not like you, not like you*

When his wife angrily tells him to 'scram be damn' to this 'wutless foolish woman', he holds up his bathing suit, and claims his innocence.

Double meaning can also be used in very serious poetry. An example is Mervyn Morris' poem *Valley Prince*, which is dedicated to Don Drummond, the Jamaican trombonist who contributed so much to early **ska** and **reggae**. Here the poet refers both to the musician's expression of a melancholy spirit through his instrument, and the fact that he died tragically in the mental hospital.

> Oonu gimme me back me trombone, man:
> is time to blow me mind

The poet suceeds in condensing a lot of meaning in a very few words. He also reverses our regular responses. We can interpret the musician's 'blowing his mind' not as madness, but as finding free musical expression at last. Challenging set ideas is a common aim of poetry.

Another way of challenging or expanding our existing ideas is through pictures conjured up in the imagination. Some of the *Negro Spiritual* songs of North America are fine poems because of the visions they contain. Death as a mighty, but welcome chariot is brought vividly to our 'inner eye' in the refrain:

> Swing low, sweet chariot
> Comin for to carry me home

'Swing', 'sweet' and 'home' all have pleasant associations for us (notice the repeated 'sw' sound) and influence our feeling about the subject of the song. We 'see' something which is friendly, soothing and familiar, rather like a baby's cradle. It turns upside down the common connections we make with death.

Martin Carter uses a vision of the sea shore to affect our thoughts about the masses of people who go hungry through poverty

> They come like sea birds
> flapping in the wake of a boat
> *(University of Hunger)*

The vision combines beauty with an idea of desperation. Why are the people like birds 'flapping'? Do we think of their arms, their hearts, their hopes? Through pictures, the poet stimulates our imagination, and encourages thoughts and questions to range freely.

We find poetry all around us. It does not only exist in books — in fact the majority of poetry is spoken or sung. We have probably all made at least fragments of poetry, playing with the sounds and meanings of words. We recognise a poet in someone who develops that pleasure into a fine and sustained art. A poet 'plays' on language — using rhythms, rhymes and other sound patterns, double meanings and so on — much as a musician draws out the possibilities of an instrument, creating a very clear and deliberate shape.

A poem can have almost any purpose. It can express such a powerful and serious meaning that it influences us permanently. It can haunt us with its beauty. It can be funny, trivial or coarse. It can even be funny and serious at the same time. Whatever the purpose, the true poet strives for the most striking or touching or memorable expression and will not be satisfied until it is found.

2 Talking about poetry

Talking about poetry is easy once you know how. But if you are not used to it, it is sometimes difficult to find the right words. You may also get put off by the words 'people in the know' seem to use. What on earth do they mean by *image* or *tone*? You may suspect that they are simply showing off. In this book, such words do not appear often, but sometimes they do seem necessary.

What people tend to do when talking about poetry is to discuss it as if it were something else, but without actually saying so. That is how you get words being used like 'structure' (as if the poem were a building) or 'texture' (as if it were a piece of cloth). Such ideas can be useful, but only if it is clear how they are being used. What we are going to do in this chapter is to try and fill in the bits which are often missed out. That is, we are going to make some comparisons that should help you understand the more difficult words used in this book.

All the difficult words, or names that need explaining are printed like this (i.e. in italics). They can be looked up in the glossary at the back. If a word or phrase printed in italics does not appear there, it means it is the title of a poem, play, etc.

The poet as a builder

A poem is pieced together, or built, like anything else that is made. In this sense it has a structure, like a building. The material it is built of is language. Poetry, like building, is a craft. To make a thing of beauty, you must understand your material thoroughly. You must know how far you can stretch it before it will buckle or crack.

If we see the poet as a builder, we must think about foundations. Caribbean poems have their own special foundations; they are built on a particular *heritage*. That heritage, as we shall consider, is made up of separate parts. In the book, these parts of the heritage are described as different *traditions*.

Kumina Queen from Jamaica. In Africa she would be called a 'guardian of the sacred word'. For most of human history, medical knowledge, religion and poetry have been passed by authorities like her by word of mouth.

A tradition is a way of doing things which becomes accepted and is handed down. The heritage of Caribbean poetry consists of two main parts: the *oral tradition* and the *literary* or *written tradition*. Both traditions have passed on poetry and stories, as well as all kinds of knowledge, including science and history. But the written tradition had the authority of the British empire behind it, and existed in books, while the oral tradition had its origins in Africa, was passed on by word of mouth, and its wisdom was in the heads of people who had no actual status in the society. Both traditions have their *literature*; in this book we call the written literature the *literary tradition*.

Caribbean poetry began on uncertain foundations. What was home-grown and familiar was supposed to be bad, while what was foreign and alien was supposed to be good. Poets could not accept this. They had to be sure of the full heritage. They wanted to work freely with all the language and other materials at their disposal. They have played an active part in getting the oral tradition properly recognised. From much more secure foundations they now feel free to experiment, and, as they hand on to younger poets, are in turn creating a new tradition of modern Caribbean poetry.

We said that the poet's material is language. In addition to the full range of *standard English*, the Caribbean poet has the special language of the region. We talk about the special possibilities in Caribbean English which the poet can use in Chapters 4, 5, and 6. When it comes to describing a particular aspect of Caribbean culture, often a Caribbean word is the only one, or certainly the best. **Caribbean words are printed like this** (i.e. in bold), at least the first time they are used. You will be familiar with them, so they need no discussion here. Whenever an English word is presented in heavy type, it is being used in its special Caribbean sense. Definitions of some Caribbean words can be found in the glossary, but your own are almost certain to be better.

The poet as photographer

A photographer captures a particular scene on his or her celluloid film. We call this an *image*. It may simply reflect the scene, or we may feel it has special meaning, and seek to *interpret* it. (For example, we may see a woman with her back to the camera and wonder about her feelings. Does she know the picture is being taken? Is she angry with the photographer? and so on.) *Image* is used in both these senses when we talk about poetry. It can mean a straightforward picture created in words, or it can mean something which requires thoughtful interpretation. Sometimes the photographer puts two things together and invites comparison. For example, people and their pet animals have been photographed in such a way that they look almost identical. Poets frequently do such things, either saying that one thing is like another ('She was as free as a bird' — a *simile*) or talking as if the subject were something else altogether ('She flew in' — a *metaphor*).

The humming bird has become a *symbol* of freedom and independence. We call an image that is used to represent something else a *metaphor*.

The photographer can also vary the degrees of light and shade and carefully select the arrangement of objects within the picture's frame to affect the 'mood' of the photograph. Similarly, the poet can use different types of words (strong or delicate, emotional or cool, for example) and arrange them in particular ways to create a particular *tone*. We all know that a person can adopt many different tones of voice when speaking (bitter, melancholy, brisk, charming). A poet can cleverly express different tones in writing.

The poet as a dreamer

Have you ever had a dream about one thing which you knew was really about something else — a terrifying wild beast confronting you, maybe — which you recognise when you wake up in the morning as that homework you are really worried about, and have avoided doing . . .? This often happens, and for this reason people like to interpret dreams. It is sometimes said that when a person dreams of a wedding, it actually means a death will take place. Even though there is no obvious connection between a wild beast and homework, or between a wedding and a death, we understand that one is a *symbol* for the other.

Somehow the experience seems more significant than if we had actually dreamed of the thing itself. Because of its powerful effect, poets often use this feature of dreams, and use a symbol which we have to interpret. Finding a meaningful connection between previously unrelated things helps us to take a fresh view of the world. Once a connection is recognised as powerful, it may be used again and again by other poets.

The *imagery* of a poem consists of images on all these levels; images as straightforward pictures, and images which have to be interpreted, like similes, metaphors and symbols. By the way, in looking at the poet as a builder, a photographer and a dreamer, we have used three metaphors. If this has helped you understand some rather difficult ideas, maybe you can begin to see the usefulness of imagery.

3 Whose voice, whose version? Caribbean poetry and the achievement of nationhood

The poetry which was written in the West Indies a hundred, even fifty, years ago may seem funny and old-fashioned to us now. We see much in the writing which stands out as imported from England and quite wrong for a Caribbean setting. We should recognise, though, what a major step it was for the early black poets simply to see themselves and commit themselves as writers against the seemingly impossible barriers of slavery and its aftermath.

If we look over the whole period of written Caribbean poetry we also see a very interesting story revealed. It is the story of a gradual takeover. At the beginning we see that the language and way of seeing things belong completely to the colonialists and local planter class. Poems emphasise loyalty to the British Empire and their language is so firmly in the tradition of English poetry that it is often hard to recognise that they are about the Caribbean at all. Everyone who received an education was soaked in this colonial viewpoint. The planter class were very comfortable with it. Descendants of slaves expressed feelings of tension in their poetry. This tension was to grow into an angry rejection of the Imperial world-view on the one hand, and a positive growth of confidence in a local vision of things on the other.

FRANCIS WILLIAMS, the first known black West Indian poet, wrote in Latin. His father, a free man, had become known in England when he petitioned for more legal rights in 1711. The English Duke of Montagu adopted Francis, who eventually went to Cambridge University. Life in England must have been difficult and confusing for him. He and one or two other black people who achieved some kind of position in England during this period must have felt relieved to have escaped the misery of slavery. Nevertheless, he was treated as a curiosity, not an equal, in the high society which was now the only world he knew. After finishing his education he returned to Jamaica. His poetry was bound to mirror his English upbringing and education, but he refused to accept the view foisted on him that his blackness made him inferior:

> Why fear, why hesitate, my blackest Muse,
> to mount the lofty palace of the
> Western Caesar? Go, greet him . . .

Despite all the barriers of prejudice which he had to overcome, he was determined to claim his status as a poet. Most significant, the spirit which inspired him – his Muse – was black. We clearly see pride, pain and turmoil present in the very foundations of Caribbean poetry.

By contrast, M.J. CHAPMAN, a white Barbadian of the planter class, writing about

Francis Williams, the first black West Indian poet, as painted by a British artist of his day. What attitude do you think the painter had towards his subject?

seventy years later, suggests that everyone in the Caribbean is living in paradise. But then one of Chapman's main aims is to argue for keeping slavery. He failed. His poem *Barbadoes* was published in 1833, the year of abolition. His example of concentrating on the beauties of the tropical vegetation and landscape were followed by other Caribbean poets for almost a century. Chapman drew on the poetry *conventions* of eighteenth-century England in which landscapes were artificial and imaginary creations.

> Fair as young Hope, and bright the lovely view,
> Crowned with its long and pillared avenue,
> Whose mountain-palms point tapering to the sky,
> While the glad rivulet brawls and babbles by

Pastoral poetry like this tends to leave out anything which is mysterious or challenging to human imagination. In Chapman's case it was a hypocritical way of shutting out reality.

It was in Guyana in the 1880s that English Caribbean poetry began to get established on a firm footing. The education the poets received blinded them to the poetry in the local songs and stories they knew, so the only model they could follow was the English one. Nevertheless, 'LEO' (real name Egbert Martin) is able to convey a genuine sense of excitement at the particular way in which light plays on a river in the Guyana forest.

> 'Tis dark but its dimples are bright as the mould,
> For a shower of sunbeams transforms them to gold;
> Transforms them to brilliants that glow, flash and quiver
>
> (from *The River*)

Poets have struggled to capture the strong Caribbean light. This schoolgirl, awaiting Princess Margaret on a visit in 1955, is only too aware of it.

The special qualities of the strong Caribbean light would continue to challenge poets. How to capture it? It needed new words, new ways of saying things. Finding words to describe the real world around was one way of taking possession of it.

The only kind of identity people in the English-speaking Caribbean were encouraged to feel was unity under the British Empire and flag. Enslaved Africans carried with them a different idea of the nation they belonged to, which was kept a cherished secret through generations. This alternative idea of nation reappears clearly in Guyanese poetry of 1888 marking fifty years since Emancipation. The poet T.R.F. ELLIOTT calls on all 'sons of Africa' to

> Join the Ethiopic hand
> In one vast, colossal band —
> In one unity, so grand,
>   As that in heaven
>   (*Emancipation Chorus*)

In Jamaica, which had a significant group of local poets by the 1920s, this kind of view took much longer to emerge in printed poetry. The Poetry League of Jamaica was founded in 1923 by J.E. CLARE MCFARLANE as a branch of the Empire Poetry League. Many of its members were of British origin and belonged to the island's elite. Their view of West Indian history concentrated on the European explorers and buccaneers, and they wrote with enthusiasm about Britain and the empire. It was their work which found a place in West Indian school readers, and was maybe part of the reason why many Caribbean students have had a rather lukewarm attitude to poetry!

TOM REDCAM (a *pseudonym*, made out of spelling his real surname MacDermot backwards) is referred to as 'the father of Jamaican poetry' and was honoured as the first Jamaican *Poet Laureate* after his death in 1933. His poetry was very highly regarded in his time and he must take first credit for bringing Jamaican poetry into being. This was not only through his own work but through his encouragement of other writers. Like other Poetry League writers, loyalty to empire is an important theme in his poetry, but he writes sincerely and with a passionate love of Jamaica which is not always so evident in the work of the others.

His contemporaries tended to disregard ordinary Jamaicans in their poems. At best, peasant folk were included as a picturesque addition to the scene. Tom Redcam makes a fisherman the hero of one of his major poems, *A Legionary of Life*.

The setting is on a grand scale: a beach of white sand overlooks a bay from which 'the reef is heard/But in faint far-off moaning, sad and low'. A river in full flood pours slowly into the sea not far from the fisherman's hut, which is flanked by 'tall grey Palms' with 'strong and sinuous trunks':

> Mid myriad empty husks and withered leaves,
> The hut stands, brown as these, with roof of straw,
> Mud walls with stones embedded, wattle-veined,
> Windows and door rough board on clumsy hinge

The language is plain by comparison with Chapman's. Only 'mid' and 'myriad' stand out as special 'poetic' words.

The fisherman's only companion is his beloved seven year old daughter. One day while they are beside the river she slips into the water. He hesitates briefly, out of fear, and by the time he plunges in she has been swept away. Although nearly drowned himself he survives and has to live not only with the pain of her loss but with a sense of guilt. Eventually the man finds 'vague soothing' for his 'deathless pain' in his familiar surroundings.

The poem succeeds because it is not over-sentimental. The fisherman is made interesting as we come to understand his very complicated feelings. This kind of long poem which tells a story is called a *narrative poem*.

As you can imagine, it is not an easy business getting poetry published. Very few people buy poetry books, so you have a hard job if you are a poet persuading any company that it would be a good idea to print and market your work. Some succeed, however, and there are a few Caribbean companies and organisations which publish on a small scale.

In the 1930s and '40s there was less support of this kind so we might conclude there was even less incentive to write poetry. However, during this period we see the emergence of groups dedicated to experimentation with writing and ideas in various parts of the Caribbean. The desire to assert a Caribbean identity, in both art and politics was gaining momentum. Some individuals were gripped with a sense of optimism which they turned to very effective and creative use. They encouraged the creative work of others and they channelled their energy into the production of magazines, among other things.

The first magazine of this kind to appear was *Trinidad* (guess where!) in 1929 which after a few issues was replaced by the *Beacon*. Their magazines were the product of a group whose interests went far wider than literature. Many of the stories which appeared marked a new departure for West Indian literature in that they concentrated on the lives of poor people and suggested that this was where the heart of Caribbean life lay. One of the most important groups of Caribbean writers were associated with the *Beacon*. These included C.L.R. James, famous internationally as a Marxist intellectual, and novelists Ralph de Boissiere and Alfred Mendes. The poetry was quite disappointing, however. The ideas were often noble, but the language was old-fashioned (even then) and clumsy.

FRANK COLLYMORE, a schoolmaster, actor and poet is remembered with affection far beyond his home of Barbados for the dynamic role he played to encourage cultural activity. He established the literary magazine *Bim* in 1942. Poets from all over the Caribbean published their work in *Bim*. This made many more people aware that a distinctive Caribbean poetry was developing. The work of the two greatest West Indian poets, Derek Walcott and Edward Kamau Brathwaite, became known to many for the first time through the magazine. Collymore encouraged high standards, mainly through his own example. Though not a great poet, his language is clear, never affected, and observant of everyday life. 'Colly' is best remembered now for his playful sketches of birds, beasts and plants, which were short and to the point:

> Christmas tidings of good cheer
> To turkeys seldom sound sincere
> (*Turkeys*)

and

> The moth
> Eath cloth
> (*The moth*)

A recent cover of *Bim,* published in Barbados. *Bim* has helped many poets to achieve recognition.

In 1943 another magazine, *Focus*, was set up in Jamaica by EDNA MANLEY, artist wife of the first Jamaican Prime Minister, Norman Washington Manley. The artist and politician in partnership were a symbol of a great convergence of political and cultural activity in the region. Together they expressed a growing sense of Caribbean nationhood. The magazine was to be a focus of all this energy.

GEORGE CAMPBELL, the major Jamaican poet of the period, saw his work first published here. Campbell's poems show his desire for clear expression rather than decoration. One reason for this is that his message has pride of place. This clarity also reflects the way objects are defined in the strong Caribbean light.

> Daylight like scarlet poinsettia
> Daylight like yellow cassia flowers
> Daylight like clean water
> Daylight like green cacti
> Daylight like sea sparkling with white horses
>
> (from *Litany*)

Great pleasure is taken from naming and noticing the beautiful things around. Previously poets had often referred to the flowers of the Caribbean as 'gaudy' because they accepted the paler, smaller flowers of Europe as the ideal, even though they clearly loved their luxuriant vegetation.

Under British colonial rule, Caribbean history, as told in the school books, was the story of Columbus, Drake and Hawkins. Information about Africa and the history of slavery was left out, as both would tarnish the brilliance of the British image. This period of growing resistance to colonialism saw an increasing determination to examine the truth of the past. VERA BELL's well-known *Ancestor on the Auction Block* was first published in a *Focus* anthology in 1948. The poem was inspired by a nationalist desire to break free from the shame and 'mental shackles' left by slavery. The poet imagines herself meeting the eyes of a black ancestor at this point of her complete humiliation, and recognises a complete person, just like herself. It is perhaps significant that Vera Bell was a near-white Creole who did not like to be called a 'black poet'. However she recognises that refusing to distance oneself from the pain of slavery is essential to the achievement of real national freedom. She views the labour of slaves as a symbol not of their degradation but of their nobility. They, and not their exploiters, are seen as the true founders of her country.

> I see you sweating, toiling, suffering
> Within your loins I see the seed
> Of multitudes
> From your labour
> Grow roads, aqueducts, cultivation
> A new country is born

In a spirit of humble dedication to these past sacrifices, the poet looks forward 'to build' the future. Vera Bell is speaking here not so much with a personal voice, but as a representative of her generation.

In Guyana (or British Guiana as it was then called) another magazine, *Kyk-over-al* began in 1946. In this case the driving spirit was the poet A.J. SEYMOUR. The magazine was named after the ruins of a Dutch fort, which form a prominent landmark over the Essequibo river.

> Kykoveral.
> Strange name for stone, a heap of stones,
> But a strong name to take imagination
> (*Over Guiana, Clouds*)

Important Guyanese contributors to the magazine were WILSON HARRIS (novelist and poet) and MARTIN CARTER (poet), as well as Seymore himself. As with *Bim*, poems and stories came from all over the Caribbean.

A.J. Seymour, like Frank Collymore, has probably been more important as a promoter of Caribbean poetry than as a poet. His work is often expansive and in this seems to reflect the grand scale of the Guyanese continental landscape. Like many other Guyanese writers he has been fascinated by the Amerindian original inhabitants, who still make a deep impact on the society. Like many of the early Jamaican writers, he is fascinated by the story of Columbus, but he brings to it a viewpoint born of the Caribbean reality and not the European myth. At the end of *For Christopher Columbus*, he considers the consequences of the historic voyage which the explorer himself could never have dreamed of. How could he know that, as a result of his voyage, 'the world was not the same'?

This sombre view of history was not surprising coming from Guyana, which suffered all kinds of upheavals and a British military occupation in the years before independence. MARTIN

CARTER was inspired to write his greatest poetry through the dreams and suffering of this time. He often knew despair

> always for me the same vision of cemetaries, slow funerals,
> broken tombs, and death designing all
> (from *Black Friday 1962*)

But even when writing in anger or bitterness, he could still show sensitivity to beauty and make images of hope:

> Sitting sometimes in the twilight near the forest
> where all the light is gone and every bird
> I notice a tiny star neighbouring a leaf
> a little drop of light a piece of glass
> straining over heaven tiny bright
> like a spark seed in the destiny of gloom
> (from *I come from the Nigger Yard*)

ERIC ROACH, of Tobago, was observing other features of the modern Caribbean. Like Martin Carter, his view and experience of the Caribbean was a very painful one. Also like Carter, he was acutely sensitive, and hope remains just a small spark of inspiration. In *Love Overgrows a Rock* he considers the physical limitations of the islands, both because of their small size and because they serve to divide the West Indian people. The physical limitations make it inevitable, he thinks, that West Indians seek to 'turn Columbus' blunder back' by travelling to 'the hostile and exploding zones' of Europe. Of course the very words he chooses show that he does not think this is any solution. During a time when many West Indian writers were travelling to Europe for the publishing opportunities and stimulation of a big international centre, Roach was deeply committed to his own home ground, and remained there. He interprets the urge to spread overseas as a great love overflowing. The image suggests the energy and creativity concentrated in the islands. It also expresses his own love, which is for the region, not simply his island. He calls on the West Indian people as to an imaginary fisherman to

> seine the archipelago;
> Disdain the sea; gather the islands' hills
> Into the blue horizons of our love

This is the image Eric Roach had in mind when he asked people to 'seine the archipelago', to draw the islands to themselves, as in an embrace.

The great love which Roach shows again and again in his poems did finally turn to despair. One day he swam out to sea and never returned.

EVAN JONES of Jamaica was one of the poets who did migrate to England, and took part in the BBC series of the 1950s, *Caribbean Voices*, which was another means by which many writers established a firm reputation. *The Song of the Banana Man* was a romantic and nostalgic view of a Jamaican small farmer. Its follow-up, *The Lament of the Banana Man*, reflects the disillusionment and hopelessness that Jones recognised in many West Indians who had migrated to England. Like many of them, the banana man probably came for a few years to make some money and return home, but now finds he 'can' go back to Jamaica now . . .' His work on the underground is meaningless to him: when he's tired of punching tickets, he simply lets people go through unchecked. The two 'banana man' poems were particularly popular because of the successful way they used the Jamaican language:

> Gal, I'm tellin you, I'm tired fo' true,
> Tired of Englan', tired o' you

Two other Caribbean poets who played a key role in shaping the *Caribbean Voices* programme were JOHN FIGUEROA and ANDREW SALKEY, both of whom have edited important *anthologies* of Caribbean poetry.

'When I'm tired o' punchin', I let dem through.' (Evan Jones, *The Lament of the Banana Man*)

A.L. HENDRICKS, from Jamaica, published two collections of calm, meditative poems of great beauty. He is one of the poets to pioneer a deceptively simple style which has become quite characteristic of modern Caribbean poetry. Hendricks' simple words express profound personal thoughts and feelings, often of a religious nature. He helped to edit *The Independence Anthology of Jamaican Literature*.

IAN McDONALD (a white Trinidadian) made his greatest impact in Guyana, where he has spent much of his life; in the theatre and as a novelist as well as being a poet. As a poet and playwright McDonald has shown a commitment to social justice. *Jaffo the Calypsonian* was one of the first really successful expressions of Trinidadian popular culture in formal poetry. Without the more obvious signs of special grammar and spelling to indicate Trinidadian speech, McDonald captures its feel through the view of the world which is portrayed.

> Jaffo was a great calypsonian, a fire ate up his soul to sing and play calypso iron-music
>
> Even when he was small he made many coloured ping-pong drums and searched them for the island music

The very long lines also reflect the way that words are often compressed into a single line of a calypso. Jaffo is an impressive figure. We are given growing hints (his 'hoarse voice', 'his clogged throat') of his developing cancer. He continues to sing, needing more and more rum to dull the pain. Even in the last month of 'hard final silence', he steals spoons from nurses in the Colonial Hospital

> to beat rhythm on his iron bedposts

The only acknowledgment of his passing comes from an Indian man who tells his story 'in a long mad chant'; his hearers simply laugh. On one level this is a very bitter poem, but the last and abiding impression is of Jaffo beating out his defiance on his spoons. The poem illustrates a generous and sensitive compassion which has been a continuing feature of McDonald's work.

ELLSWORTH McG. ('SHAKE') KEANE of St Vincent was also experimenting with language — using standard English but organising it in ways which he felt reflected the Caribbean reality. He is a jazz musician, and his music and poetry have been closely connected. He published regularly in *Bim* from its early days. His *Fragments and Patterns* is precisely what it says — fragments of people's speech and of his own experience which promise to make patterns but yet always remain fragments. Can you see how close this is to Eric Roach's view of the islands — that they form a pattern and yet remain fragments? But Keane has used words like musical sound and patterns on the page instead of Roach's more traditional way of making meaning. The words gather momentum as a pattern

> Once the sea
> Said to the wind
> I am sad
>   Heed me
> I am unwanted
>   Need me

and then break off and change into something else. The end of the poem is made up of fragments, but its last word, 'History', suggests another kind of pattern. (We turn the past into 'history' by seeing certain patterns in it.)

> And out of a pattern of blood
> We
>   Oh my islands . . .
> And out of a pattern of tides and blood
> History.

West Indian poets by now were beginning to feel free to experiment with language in any way they chose. In this chapter we have looked at the possibilities offered by the written tradition as it was inherited from Britain, and how it was transformed by Caribbean writers as their desire to express independent identity got stronger. In the next chapter we shall look at another tradition to which more and more poets are strongly connected — the language and literature which lives in people's memories and on their tongues.

Exercises

1. Pay a visit to the biggest library you can get to. With the help of the librarian, look for any books or pamphlets of Caribbean poetry printed before 1960. List them in two ways: first by date, beginning with the earliest, and second by the country in which they are printed. Are any printed locally, and if so, by which companies? See if they are still printing books. By making a few enquiries you may be able to uncover the history of poetry in print in your area.
2. Consider the different possibilities for bringing poetry to the public in your country. These will include newspapers, school magazines, the radio and TV, festivals and concerts. Do you think there are enough openings for poets?
3. See if you can paint a picture about light — the dapples and sunbeams of forest and shade, or the brilliance of the unsheltered open.
4. Imagine Christopher Columbus returning to the Caribbean in the twentieth century. What would he make of the events which followed his voyage? What would you say to him?
5. Topics for essays and discussion.
   a) 'Problems faced by the early Caribbean poets.'
   b) 'Why did poetry and politics come together in the independence movement?'
   c) 'The Caribbean's own special beauty.'

4 The people's language

Poetry has been known and enjoyed all over the world since ancient times. Reading and writing were skills known only to a few until about 150 years ago. So it follows that most of the world's poetry has been passed on by word of mouth. In some societies today (Somalia in Africa, for example), the finest poetry comes out of the *oral tradition*.

In the Caribbean a new oral tradition developed, created first by Africans in the strange tongue of their European captors. They brought to this language African humour, ways of saying things, and ways of looking at the world. It helped people to survive. Even though this **creole** language was looked down on by the slave masters, it became stronger as the people made it their own.

When people look for the early poems of the Caribbean they tend to look for what has been written. But there were more poems to be found within the oral tradition, mostly in the form of songs.

> Dis long time gal me never see yuh
> Come mek me hol yuh han
>
> Peel head John Crow
> Siddung pun tree top
> Pick off de blossom
> Mek me hol yuh han gal
> Mek me hol yuh han

This song has *imagery* as deep as any written poem. The John Crow (an image of death) casts a shadow over young love, picking off the blossoms which symbolise new life and hope.

Because this oral tradition was officially ignored, people used to find it difficult to imagine that serious poetry could be composed in **dialect** (see glossary). CLAUDE MCKAY, of Jamaica, was one of the first West Indian poets to use dialect in his work. He published two volumes of poems in 1912 before leaving Jamaica, never to return. He never wrote another poem in the first language of his childhood, either, although he often wrote in a nostalgic way about his birthplace.

Claude McKay in policeman's uniform. He soon left the force, finding he had too much sympathy with the people he was supposed to regard as criminal.

In fact, it was always his ambition to write in a traditional English poetic style. His most well-known poems are *sonnets*. It was, ironically, an English friend, Walter Jekyll, who persuaded him to write in the Jamaican dialect, suggesting he could become 'the *Robbie Burns* of Jamaica'.

McKay's poems are a landmark in the history of Caribbean poetry, and many are important for what they say and reveal about life in Kingston at that time. They also reflect an absolute faith in the values of the country people, which was something quite new in poetry. But you often feel that he is straining against the language, trying to make it more 'poetic' by making it less Jamaican! The result can sound very awkward:

> Dere by de woodland let me build my home
> Where tropic roses ever are in bloom
> (*The Hermit*)

His poems are most successful where he puts the words into the mouth of another character whom he regards as 'low class'. Then he feels no need to be polite, and as a result the language is more lively and sounds much more convincing:

> Say wha'? — res me? — you go to hell!
> You t'ink Judge don't know unno well?
> You t'ink him gwine go sentence me
> Widout a soul fe witness i?
> (*A Midnight Woman to the Bobby*)

See here how much closer the language is to natural speech in rhythms and choice of words, and how McKay uses the African word **unno** instead of 'you'.

To a large extent, Claude McKay's poetry stems directly from the *oral tradition*. He was born in the country and grew up surrounded by a rich rural culture, which you can read about in his fascinating *autobiography*, *My Green Hills of Jamaica*. When he started to write his poems in **creole**, his only models were the folk songs he had heard all his life. So his poems were naturally called *Songs* and *Ballads*. He even composed tunes for some of them.

Coming from the country to the city of Kingston was a shock for him. Working as a policeman, he witnessed the constant injustice which ruled the lives of poor people. His dialect poems are now available in print once more. If you can get hold of a copy, perhaps you could compare the conditions he described with those in your own capital.

McKay almost always talked about the bad side of city life. He may have been unaware of the first beginnings of an urban culture which was to provide inspiration and a 'voice' for many later poets.

Artists, who were very popular, but not taken very seriously by their society at the time, were developing all kinds of expression — poetry, songs, skits — often performed in an improvised **yard theatre**. They were not concerned to impress high society with their 'good English', but wanted to share their opinions and experiences with ordinary people like themselves in the language they all knew, and which vividly expressed their own lives. It was a continuation of older traditions, but it was organised in a new way — as variety acts in Kingston, or calypso tents in Port of Spain. Audiences had a chance to sit back, laugh, and enjoy hearing their own language being used wittily by the performers.

One young girl who would have been enjoying some of these acts during the 1930s in Kingston was Louise Bennett, who has become Jamaica's most beloved poet/performer, known to all as Miss Lou. Marcus Garvey first gave a platform to the comedian and storyteller, Ranny Williams, and the duo Slim and Sam, who sang topical songs and extolled the virtues of Garveyism. These shows were harrassed by the authorities and were regarded by 'respect-

Ernest Cupidon's production of H.G. de Lisser's *Jane's Career* in the 1930s. Cupidon is the 'woman' on the far left!

able' society as 'low entertainment'.

Cupidon was an extremely gifted actor and comedian who made a reputation in Europe as well as the Caribbean. He was most famous for his impersonations of women. He brought Jamaican **dialect** into 'respectable' theatre for the first time.

It was such acts which inspired the independent-minded young Louise, who was a

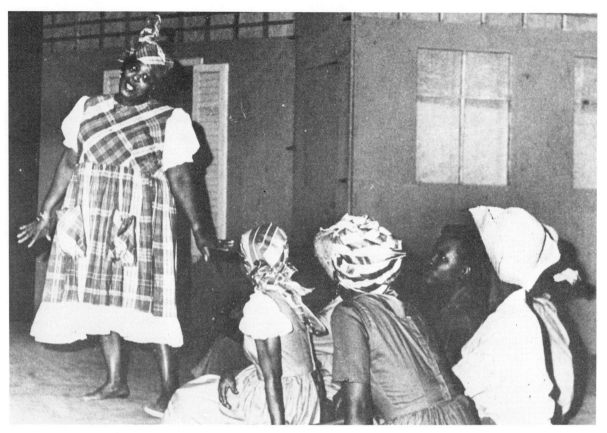

A young Miss Lou in the Jamaican pantomime *Anancy and Dombey*.

natural comedienne and performer. She had also been given a book of McKay poems once as a school prize, which provided a model for her writing. She started performing while still a school student at variety shows organised by Eric Coverley, who was later to become her husband.

Like Claude McKay, Louise Bennett's themes have come directly from the experiences of ordinary people in country and town. Like him, too, she used her poetry to express pride in being black; as here, where she describes her feelings at a performance of Marion Anderson, a black singer from the United States:

> Me head tun gig, me heart swell big,
> Me proud, me please, me glad;
> Me look pon her, den look dung pon
> Me han, an seh 'Teng Gad'.
> (*Monday Gawn*)

Miss Bennett's presence on stage is warm and motherly, and she has always inspired great affection from her audiences, as far afield as Trinidad, London and Toronto. Her predecessors in variety performance often presented characters to be laughed at, but Louise Bennett celebrates her characters — not as heroes necessarily, but as people to be loved. She has been important in encouraging others, by example, to write, perform and enjoy **dialect** poetry.

Because she is so popular now, on TV and radio as well as the stage, it is difficult to imagine that she had a hard time gaining acceptance. She always described herself as a writer first, but it was many years before her poems appeared in print.

They were just not taken seriously. The reflex response was to laugh, dismissively, and pay little attention to what was being said. Yet many of her satirical poems make serious points about people's prejudices and short-comings, or talk in a sensitive and involved way about hardship. *Dutty Tough*, widely regarded as one of her best poems, is not funny at all:

> Sun a shine an pot a bwile, but
> Tings no bright, bickle no nuff.
> Rain a fall, river dah flood, but
> Water scarce and dutty tough.

By referring to the sun and rain, Miss Lou points out that there should be abundant food. She contrasts this with the actual shortage of water and the hard ground which yields little produce. These contrasts are balanced in an old-time pro-verbial style which suggests strength and patience in the speaker without diminishing the sense of basic injustice.

All the younger poets who write and perform most of the time in **dialect** acknowledge inspiration from Miss Lou. The one who probably learned most directly is PAUL KEENS-DOUGLAS, of Trinidad and Grenada. He studied drama in Jamaica, and since becoming established as an artist, has performed with Miss Bennett on many occasions.

He has performed a similar role in the East Caribbean, encouraging people to enjoy and appreciate their spoken language. Like her, he has worked extensively in school, much to the delight of students and most teachers, although there are still some people who feel very uncomfortable about non-standard English being used in a school context.

Although he is widely known as a 'dialect poet', the rhythms he uses often sound closer to the prose of story-telling than to verse. This is especially true when he adds spontaneous comments in performance (two of his special talents are: rapport with an audience, and comic timing). Here, in *All Fall Down*, Paul prepares to launch into a piece of 'ole talk':

> Miss Maisie when ah tell yu,
> Big fight break out last night.
> Yes, ah mean big, big fight.
> Was a real scandal, but ah enjoy it, yu hear?

Most importantly, he has helped people to recognise and enjoy the poetic qualities of their everyday speech. For example, the easy coinage of *similes*:

> She mouth did set like ten rat trap

and other vivid *imagery*:

> Dey say Sugar cut he navel string
> On a Esso drum dat still have oil,
> For, as long as day could remember, Sugar was beatin' pan — all kind ah pan.
> (*Sugar George*)

Such images form a natural part of the conversational style. It is certain we can thank the calypso tradition for the witty and creative speech which is one of Trinidad's best treasures.

BRUCE ST. JOHN, from Barbados, is best known for his poetry in the **bajan** dialect. He has tended, like Bennett and Keens-Douglas, to work within a humorous range, but he was originally motivated by the political consciousness awakened by the Black Power movement.

He often uses the call-and-response style which is commonly heard in black churches. He also employs many *proverbs*. In *Bajan Litany* he suggests that his country is rather prone to

Bruce St. John

imitate others, not always to its advantage:

Follow pattern kill Cadogan.	Yes, Lord.
America got black power?	O Lord.
We got black power	Yes, Lord.
Wuh sweeten goat mout bun 'e tail.	O Lord

How would you *interpret* the two proverbs Bruce St. John uses here?

We will be considering the work of the **dub poets** in Chapter 6: *Poems of Protest*. Their poetry draws mainly on urban traditions, especially reggae music. MICHAEL SMITH, though called a dub poet, also drew much inspiration from the other rural traditions of song and proverbs. It is a bitter tragedy that this gifted young man was murdered, at a time when his talents were beginning to be recognised outside his native Jamaica.

Like Louise Bennett, he was intensely aware of the things people — old or young, from country or city — say. His poems are full of songs, children's games, nursery rhymes and snatches of vivid conversation. *Mi Cyaan Believe It*, the poem which brought him considerable fame, draws much of its power from the constant repetition of the *title phrase*. Michael Smith heard this phrase often as he stood at a bus stop or moved from place to place. For him, and for those who were moved by the poem, it seemed to sum up the people's state of mind in the face of hopeless conditions.

Another Smith poem, *Roots*, sums up the whole direction of Miss Bennett's life work; the wish for people

> t'accept dem blackness
> . . .
> t'accept dem blackness
> an
> others/as they are

So we can clearly see a continuity of feeling and purpose in this poetry which is rooted in the oral tradition. In Chapters 3 and 4 we have now looked at the two major 'tributaries' — oral and written — which form the mainstream of Caribbean literature.

Exercises

1. There are sadly very few records of early popular entertainers. See what your oldest relatives can remember about names, details of acts, venues, etc. Better still, can they remember songs? Do they have newspaper clippings? You could turn this into a class project, and later present your findings to the local library. They could become a valuable resource.
2. Choose someone to read Louise Bennett's *Dutty Tough* with as much emphasis and feeling as possible. Discuss the feelings you experience when you hear something serious performed in **dialect**.
3. Make a collection of poems in your own local language. (You should find poems in newspapers and local magazines if there are few books available.) You could then run a competition to see who can give the best performance of any poem in your anthology.
4. Think of some local words or expressions which are unique to your country or parish. See if you can compose a poem around one or more of them.
5. Topics for essays or discussion.
   a) 'The importance of Louise Bennett's or Paul Keens-Douglas' poetry.'
   b) 'The special qualities of West Indian spoken language.'
   c) 'Appropriate uses of standard English and **dialect**.'
   d) 'Town talk and country talk.'

5 Brathwaite and Walcott – poets national and international

DEREK WALCOTT and EDWARD KAMAU BRATHWAITE are internationally recognised as major poets currently writing in English. They have received several important arts awards in the United States and Britain. Readings by the poets are regarded as important events and their work is studied in schools and universities in Africa, the United States and several European countries.

Yet they are first and foremost Caribbean writers. Both poets' work reflects a struggle with the English language to make it truthfully reflect the Caribbean experience. Writers from the Caribbean, from Africa, India, even Australia, have faced problems in how they use English. How do you refashion the language of a former colonial power, full of prejudices, and values based on life in another part of the planet, so that it can express your own, completely different, 'world'? How can you use it freshly and creatively, independent of its British origins? Brathwaite and Walcott, in their different ways, have made an important contribution to Caribbean English. They have used the full range of the language, from **dialect** to *standard English*, to exhibit its richness. Brathwaite's work, in particular, gave poetry a popularity it had never previously enjoyed in the West Indies, and encouraged poets who expressed themselves best in dialect to do so.

Both poets have helped to teach an international readership to appreciate Caribbean expressions and viewpoints. While responding

Derek Walcott

to cultural developments in different parts of the world, both poets have at the same time remained very local in their concerns. The majority of their work is concerned with people and places of the Caribbean. Just as students from the Caribbean have to do a lot of work to picture, say, the landscape described in a poem by the English *Romantic* poet, William Wordsworth, so students from outside the Caribbean have to work to know what seagrapes or

21

'galvanise' look like, or to begin to understand the viewpoints being expressed. Yet international students make the effort because they are excited by a fresh use of English which promises new understandings.

Edward Kamau Brathwaite

Brathwaite and Walcott would not have been able to develop as Caribbean poets to the extent they have without the legacy of George Campbell, Louise Bennett, Martin Carter, Frank Collymore, Eric Roach and others who helped to establish a Caribbean 'voice', as we discussed in Chapter 3. In their early years of apprenticeship and experiment, they were a part of this continuing search.

The period of English history which produced the seagoing explorers and buccaneers who plundered the Caribbean also produced a very energetic new English and a great deal of poetry. The Caribbean was associated with high romance in the English imagination. As we saw in Chapter 3, this view strongly influenced earlier Caribbean poets and was heavily promoted through the poetry anthologies used in schools when Walcott was young. Walcott used this heritage, but always with a strong sense of *irony*. He belonged to a new generation which was probing and questioning the colonial viewpoint. The young Walcott was drawn to the energetic language of sixteenth and seventeenth century England, as it seemed to reflect some of the brilliance of his St Lucia environment. He was, however, intensely aware that the English *literary tradition* was the creation of the people who had enslaved his ancestors, and who combined their idealism with greed and cruelty. In one poem, Walcott describes his exploration of the ruins of a Great House, which for him symbolise the demise of the British empire.

> . . . pacing, I thought next
> Of men like Hawkins, Walter Raleigh, Drake,
> Ancestral murderers and poets, more perplexed
> In memory now by every ulcerous crime
> (from *Ruins of a Great House*)

A ruined Great House like this aroused the anguished emotions expressed in Derek Walcott's poem.

Raleigh was a poet and adventurer, Drake a buccaneer and Hawkins a slave trader. Though actions like theirs brought catastrophe on Africa and the Americas, the English tradition immortalised them as heroes. Walcott battled with the problem of how he could grow as a poet through language and literature which he loved without being destroyed by this version of history.

Walcott drew deeply on the *oral traditions* of St Lucia in his early plays (*Ti Jean and his Brothers* — actually in *verse* — *Malcochon* and *Dream on Monkey Mountain*). These are full of folk heroes and supernatural characters, yet address themselves in a radical way to contemporary issues in the Caribbean. They also make creative use of the St Lucia **patois**. However, apart from the drama, his poetry for more than twenty years drew on Western European literary tradition for its major symbols.

The young Edward Brathwaite was drawn to the twentieth-century cultural movements of North America in his search for his own voice as a poet. He was particularly affected by Black American jazz, which challenged traditional European musical ideas, and the poetry of T.S. Eliot. Eliot, although seen as an English poet, revealed his American roots through the conversational way in which he wrote. He also broke away from the special 'poetic' vocabulary typical of English poetry. It is a *paradox* that Brathwaite, who studied in England, should have been drawn closer to the Americas in terms of style and viewpoint, while Walcott, who never left the Caribbean until his maturity, should have looked to Europe for inspiration. Why do you think this could be?

Brathwaite felt that jazz was a release of the true voice of Black people in the Americas. He argued that 'jazz features' could be identified in the work of Caribbean writers, such as the novelist, Roger Mais. His efforts to reflect jazz form in his poetry — breaking up formal structures, and creating continual 'surprises' in the way he uses or arranges words — have remained constant features of his work.

The two poets responded very differently to the Black Power movement of the 1960s. Brathwaite, who had lived for eight years in Ghana, West Africa, felt completely at home with the demand for an 'Africanization' of the society. His poem cycle, *The Arrivants*, drew on understandings gained in Africa to explore Caribbean identity in a more confident and optimistic way. It seemed to answer a deeprooted desire to throw off European cultural domination. But it was sections like the one quoted below which probably drew the most immediate response from readers and audiences. The harsh tone of the Rastafarian speaker seems to have more in common with the exploded rage of Black America than the calmer reflections of traditional West African philosophy.

> So beat dem burn
> dem, learn
> dem dat dem
> got dem nothin'
> but dem
> bright bright baubles
> (from *Wings of a Dove*)

The repetition of 'dem' draws on a feature of Jamaican speech. Here it is exaggerated to achieve a deliberate effect. What do you think that effect is?

Walcott however accused Black Power advocates of trying to simplify the Caribbean situation. He had founded the Trinidad Theatre Workshop in 1956, and his years in that country made him acutely conscious of the Indo-Caribbean identity.

> sometimes bald clouds in saffron robes assemble
> sacred to the evening,
> sacred even to Ramlochan,
> singing Indian hits from his jute hammock
> while evening strokes the flanks
> and silver horns of his maroon taxi
> (from *The Saddhu of Couva*)

The Earl Hines Orchestra of 1938. E.K. Brathwaite regards jazz sounds as a true New World Black voice, finally released.

Derek Walcott spent many years in Trinidad, where he was touched by the Indo-Caribbean experience. This young East Indian worker, like Ramlochan in Walcott's *The Saddhu of Couva*, is very much a part of the modern Caribbean.

As usual, Walcott is making the point that the Caribbean is a mixture of cultures. Ramlochan is surrounded by echoes of his Indian heritage, yet he is firmly rooted in a modern West Indian commercial situation. He feels an almost traditional reverence towards his maroon taxi, which is clearly his pride and joy. Walcott frequently makes a point about his own mixed blood, which he sees as neither a source of pride nor shame. For Brathwaite, however, the key point remains

> Ninety-five per cent of my people poor
> ninety-five per cent of my people black
> (from *Caliban*)

What does he mean by 'my people'?

Walcott makes few references to African tradition in his poetry. In *Laventille* he denies any continuity with the African past

> We left
> somewhere a life we never found,
> customs and gods that are not born again,
> some crib, some grill of light
> clanged shut on us in bondage

Despite important differences of emphasis, however, the two poets have often drawn on similar sources of inspiration.

Both pay homage to friends and family. Walcott's epic poem, *Another Life*, is an *autobiography* in verse. Friends, family and the natural environment are the strongest influences on his early development. As Walcott thinks of his widowed mother he recreates in imagination the world of quiet, order and controlled pain over which she presided. The Sunday silence is contrasted with the weekday sound of the Victrola sewing machine. Her husband's fading watercolours fill the room with echoes of the past:

> Maman,
> you sat folded in silence,
> as if your husband might walk up the street,
> while in the forests the cicadas pedalled their machines,
> and silence, a black maid in white,
> barefooted, polished and repolished
> the glass across his fading water-colours,
> the dumb Victrola cabinet
> (from Chapter 2, *Another Life*)

What is the effect of the phrase, '. . . the cicadas pedalled their machines'? One of Walcott's gifts has been his ability to summon up commonplace images (such as the woman at the sewing machine), bringing vividly to life scenes typical of the Caribbean in such a way that, once recognised, they can never again be taken for granted.

Some of Brathwaite's relatives have also become symbols in his poetry. In his long *Mother Poem*, the subject is a fusion of the poet's mother, all Caribbean mothers and the poet's motherland, Barbados. In *Ogun*, he sug-

Nigerian masks in their context as part of a communal ceremony. Have you seen anything like them in the Caribbean? Where do you think the uncle in Brathwaite's *Ogun* got the inspiration for his carving?

gests an explanation for the mysterious carving which his uncle, a carpenter and cabinet maker, commits himself to so devotedly in his spare time. The product is a disturbing, and unmistakeably African, carved mask:

> dry shuttered
> eyes, slack, anciently everted lips, flat
> ruined face

Why do you think the face is 'ruined'? The artist, free of the demands of the customer, instinctively explores the nature of the wood he handles. The wood evokes for him a world he has never experienced; the forests of his ancestral home.

> And as he cut, he heard the creak of forests:
> green lizard faces gulped, grey memories with moth
> eyes watched him from their shadows, soft
> liquid tendrils leaked among the flowers
> and a black rigid thunder he had never heard within his hammer
> came stomping up the trunks

The uncle, only dimly aware of what he creates, is nevertheless gripped with a sense of purpose which Brathwaite believes comes from the African Yoruba god, Ogun. The carving is described as the 'emerging woodwork image of his anger'. How do you interpret the 'black rigid thunder'?

Both Brathwaite and Walcott grew up in small islands, where the sea is always at hand. The sea has provided a focus for meditation and a wealth of imagery drawn from shoreline to horizon. The seascape has alternatively suggested confinement and isolation; taking possession through naming and describing things; dreams and escape; separation between past and present, or a link with continental Africa.

Walcott used the image of Robinson Crusoe, cast up on a Caribbean island, to examine his feelings of isolation. Out of necessity he learns to know and love the seascape, and gradually his thoughts and feelings begin to reflect the shapes, worn to purity by sun, wind and water, that lie around him. He decides

> To let a salt sun scour
> The brain as harsh as coral
> To bathe like stones in wind
> To be, like beast or natural object, pure.

Brathwaite similarly describes a sightless fisherman reduced to simplicity by the elements, just like the objects on the beach

> his eyes stare out like an empty shell,
> its sockets of voices, wind,
> grit, bits of conch, pebble

But the fisherman 'has his voices'. Like the carpenter/artist in *Ogun*, the fisherman is aware of things beyond his immediate world because he is so in tune with his natural environment. Both poets have looked to the sea shore in the search for knowledge out of simple things.

Schooners appear frequently in Walcott's poems. In one sense they represent the way the poet has come to know the Caribbean, the links between the separate islands. They can also promise escape. A recent long poem of Walcott's is entitled *The Schooner Flight*, which describes a sea-journey in the schooner *Flight* by a sailor called Shabine. The journey is in fact no escape, but a series of dramatic and dangerous encounters, from which Shabine emerges wiser, but not unscathed. In one of these, Shabine encounters a ghostly fleet

> We float through a rustling forest of ships
> with sails dry like paper, behind the glass
> I saw men with rusty eyeholes like cannons

At the back are slave ships, but Shabine is deprived the sight of any of his ancestors:

> our fathers below deck too deep, I suppose
> to hear us shouting. So we stop shouting

The sea thus represents history, and the link with the African past, always marred by the terrible Middle Passage. The eastern horizon represents the gateway to the past, hence a common Walcott *image*: 'the mind halved by a horizon'.

When Brathwaite looks at the Americas, dominated by neon lights, banana companies and high rise buildings, he too concludes: 'The sea is a divider. It is not a life-giver' (from *Jah*). However, he perceives another Caribbean separate from the harsh vitality of American commerce. Somewhere within this simpler way, an African spirit, however unrecognised, remains, especially in communities attached to the sea:

> The streets' root is in the sea
> in the deep harbours;
> it is a long way from Guinea
> but the gods still have their places;
> they can walk up out of the sea
> into our houses
> <div align="right">(from <i>Shepherd</i>)</div>

Brathwaite uses images from the sea to suggest growth and beginnings. Barbados, his home, is a coral island, which has gradually grown up out of the sea

> The land rises slowly
>   fed by the ringed sun and the distant Amazon
> <div align="right">(from <i>Coral</i>)</div>

The coral begins from a grain of sand in the eye of a small sea-creature, the polyp. From small and hidden origins come the foundations of an island, and this becomes a symbol for the Caribbean people

The sea means many things to many people. To some it is a source of livelihood . . .

. . . to others it is a place for fun and exitement . . .

>   a fist curled
> in embryo slowly uncurling

Brathwaite also associates the sea with childhood, happiness and adventure. Adam, the central character of his *Sun Poem*, is a 'landboy' who wants to be one of the 'beachboys', and proves himself by winning an underwater struggle with Batto, 'the boast of the beachboys gang'. As a boy, the water is as familiar an element to Adam as the land

> he knew he wouldnt lose time nor his way
>
> which was lighted and bright like a road on a moonlight night
>
> dips and hills he passed that were smooth or covered with moss
> and the sand was ribbed like water in wind
> and all was as silent as a
> fish-eye look

The sea as described here is still mysterious, but offers also a sense of joy and freedom.

Let us look finally at ways in which the poets have worked at their language to make it express more closely their thoughts and feelings. Although Walcott's first international publication *In A Green Night* is remembered for its brilliance of language and its wealth of *allusions* to European literature, he states his ambitions as a writer simply:

> I seek
> As climate seeks its style, to write
> Verse crisp as sand, clear as sunlight
> Cold as the curled wave, ordinary
> As a tumbler of island water
> (from *Islands*)

The language became plainer and plainer as he sought to give sharp detail to his experience of the Caribbean. His early poetry uses traditional English structures, including the *sonnet*. These provided good discipline for a young poet still developing his craft, but often the patterns of rhythm and stress worked against the rhythms of Caribbean English, so that his early use of dialect in his poetry contrasted with its rather foreign context. The lines of his most recent poetry remain very carefully controlled, but the exact pattern depends on meaning rather than any pre-determined system. The language now often moves gently in and out of the dialect, using other people's speech, distinctive Caribbean expressions, and a slight vagueness about past and present tense, to create a distinctive 'Walcott voice'.

> . . . my hair grip my skull,
> it was horrors, but it was beautiful.
> We float through a rustling forest of ships
> (from *The Schooner Flight*)

From his early poetry, Brathwaite was breaking up words and lines as he sought to capture the sense of jazz music. He was also characterised as a poet who used dialect, even though most of *The Arrivants* is in standard English. Many of the most memorable pieces were in dialect.

> how you? How
> you, Eveie, chile?
> You tek dat Miraculous Bush
> fuh de trouble you tell me about?
> (from *The Dust*)

He was also attracted to words with sounds that suggested more than one meaning, and he played around with these. He describes the Caribbean islands as

> hump-
> backs out of the eye
> lands, my is-
> lands
> (from *Dawn*)

Brathwaite has taken inspiration from Rastafarian sound-fusions. One such is the fusion of I/eye, which suggests the individual is a see-er and a visionary. (Now he might have written is-lands as I-lands.) Increasingly Brathwaite has freely changed words, challenging our fixed view of things.

> shattering the rain/blow
> (from *Indigone*)

suggests an act of tremendous violence against something delicate while at the same time giving the rainbow its own explosive quality. These very few words also give a sense of the wind, rain and other elements which create the rainbow.

Both Walcott and Brathwaite continue to excite us with new vision and new achievements in language with every volume of poems they produce. They have both made very practical contributions to the foundations of Caribbean literature — Walcott as a playwright and theatre director, Brathwaite as a publisher of the magazine *Savacou*. Their achievements are growing and lasting ones. All Caribbean poets can now begin from the security of a firm-based tradition.

Exercises

1. Read Brathwaite's poem *Ogun*. Make drawings, paintings or sculptures of
   a) the carpenter uncle;
   b) the mask he carves;
   c) the African forest he imagines;
   d) Ogun, the African god.
   Compare the images you make with those made by your classmates.
2. Have you ever explored the ruins of a Great House or other old building full of echoes of the past? Write a poem or story which shows the effect it had on your imagination and feelings.
3. Make up word-sketches of 'characters' (past and present) talked about in your family or community, putting emphasis on their special qualities and/or achievements. When people talk about the past it is called oral history. A group of you could record

the oral history of your community.
4. Draw a map of the Caribbean and then plot an imaginary journey by sea. Write a story (a narrative poem perhaps) of what you see and experience. Read it aloud and discuss possible ways of dramatising it, using sound effects and mime.
5. Read Walcott's poem, *The Saddhu of Couva*. Sketch or paint
   a) The Saddhu
   b) Ramlochan;
   c) Couva village;
   d) the India which echoes in the Saddhu's imagination.
6. Topics for essays or discussion.
   a) Discuss 'what the sea means to me'. You could use some of these ideas: a link with the rest of the Caribbean; a link with the land of my ancestors; isolation and confinement; a break with the past; escape; a source of peace and tranquility; a place for fun and adventure; a place of work.
   b) Do you think Caribbean poets should aim for international recognition? Discuss the advantages, both for the poet and his/her audience. Can you see any drawbacks?
   c) Take a poem by Brathwaite or Walcott (suggestions *Lix* or *Shabine Encounters the Middle Passage*) in which a range of different kinds of English are used. Try to mark them out and describe them (as **dialect** or **nation language**, old-fashioned English, teacher- or sailor-talk, standard English and any other ways you can think of). Can you say how the different types of language make the poem more interesting?

6 Poems of protest

We could call Anancy the original hero of West Indian literature. Like the majority of his successors, his ancestor was African: the trickster spider hero of Ghanaian popular tales. Anancy survived the Middle Passage in the hearts and minds of those who had created him, and, like them, he had to adapt to drastically changed circumstances under slavery. In the stories he survives because he is humorous, flexible and sharp, but this does not disguise the fact that his environment is uncertain and dangerous. This is vividly brought home to us in a story where Anancy confronts Brother Death himself, and has to bargain with the lives of his whole family. Do you know it, or one like it?

The literature of the Caribbean is born in the context of this struggle against unchosen circumstances. The arrival of East Indians was hardly more voluntary that that of Africans; this time forced by poverty rather than the slaver's gun.

It is therefore not surprising that the spirit of protest has been central to the development of Caribbean literature. Have you ever thought of the traditional song, *Linstead Market* as a protest poem? The narrator has failed to sell even a 'quattie-wut' of ackee on market day:

> Lawd, what a night, not a bite
> What a Satidee night . . .

These same words are echoed in MICHAEL SMITH's **dub poem**, *Mi Cyaan Believe It*, along with other phrases from songs and games reflecting life as a hard struggle. Think of some of the old songs and ring games you know. You will find the words of many of them are not at all lighthearted.

Almost all the modern poets have demonstrated a sharp awareness of social problems in their poetry. But there are some poets we associate particularly with what we call committed writing — writing which is not about the personal feelings of the author, but which seeks to influence social attitudes. GEORGE CAMPBELL made the social conditions of Jamaica almost his only subject. He was deeply involved in the 'troubles' of 1937–8, which rocked the Caribbean with protests against poverty and unemployment, and with the spirit of nationalism. Another political activist who is also a fine poet is MARTIN CARTER, of Guyana, whose best work was inspired by the bitter independence struggle of the 1950s. These two poets provided major inspiration for the *protest tradition* of the Caribbean.

A family of East Indian indentured labourers in 1896. Neither Africans nor Indians came exactly willingly to the Caribbean.

Some common themes of protest poetry

We find a very different kind of landscape being portrayed from the romantic *pastorals* of many early poets. It is one of extreme harshness, reflecting the most cruel aspects of life. The sun reduces features to stark simplicity, here echoed in the language of GEORGE CAMPBELL's *History Makers*.

> Hard white piles
> Of stone
> Under hot sky

This poem celebrates the women who break stones to surface the roads. Like the landscape, there is a sense in which their feelings are dried up: 'No smiles/No sigh/No moan'.

We do not often consider DEREK WALCOTT as a protest poet, yet his *Laventille* belongs firmly to the protest tradition. Laventille is Port of Spain's poorest district, established by thousands of ex-slaves immediately after emancipation. The landscape Walcott sees consists of 'steel tinkling' in the heat. Beneath these roofs, 'inheritors of the middle passage stewed'. This 'sea' of roofs is related in the poet's mind to the sea route by which his ancestors arrived, and through this image, Walcott unites the experience of all Caribbean people, past and present:

> climbing, we could look back
> with widening memory
> on the hot, corrugated iron sea
> whose horrors we all
> shared

Laventille, Port of Spain.

Again, the landscape (or 'seascape') portrayed is hard and harsh. Walcott directs his protest against the cruelty of history, which he sees as a tyrannical force.

The eccentric or mad person has always had a prominent place in the poetry of protest. They are often portrayed as sensitive or independent minded people who highlight social madness around them. In HEATHER ROYES *Theophilus Jones*, the hero of the poem liberates himself finally from the pressures of society by walking naked through the main street of Kingston before drowning himself in the harbour.

His act is a savage accusation towards a society which has afforded him no place.

In SLADE HOPKINSON's poem, *The Madwoman of Papine*, the woman adopts a position which symbolises the state of her world:

> with hanging arms, still feet,
> chin on breast, forehead parallel
> to the eroded, indifferent earth

Her pose forms a timeless, wordless protest, like the action of Theophilus Jones.

Colonial conditioning transmitted in the past through the education system is also a cause for protest. The MIGHTY SPARROW had an enormous impact throughout the Caribbean with his calypso, *Dan is the Man in the Van*. This used a series of nonsense rhymes drawn from Nelson's *West Indian Readers* (written by an Englishman called Capt. J.O. Cutteridge) to illustrate their thoughtless irrelevance to the needs of West Indian children.

> They beat me like a dog to learn that in school
> If my head was bright I woulda be a damn fool

These readers dominated the lives of every school child. You may think your own school life is less than perfect, but if you have heard anything from older members of your family about their school days, you will know you have much to thank Sparrow for!

Nursery rhymes enjoyed a new popularity when they were taken up, mainly for their sound and rhythmic value, into the repertoire of

Can a big pig dance.
Can a pig dance a jig.
A big pig can dance a jig in
  a wig for a fig.
Tim and Tot can dance for
  a fig. Have you a fig. No.

A page from the reader that inspired the Mighty Sparrow's calypso, *Dan is the Man in the Van*. Think of at least two reasons why it provoked Sparrow's scorn.

the dub DJs. Once again, they became material for protest, this time to illustrate the gap between people's fantasies and their reality. In *Nursery Rhyme Lament*, MUTABARUKA queries whether time has brought true progress:

> first time
> jack & jill
> used to run up de hill everyday
> now dem get pipe . . . an
> water rate increase

Prison also features in the poetry of protest since, as Derek Walcott puts it, poor people's lives so often 'revolve around prison, graveyard, church'. A significant number of the poets are, in any case, writing from personal experience. MARTIN CARTER's *On the Fourth Night of Hunger Strike* is powerful because he writes as he is engaged in a protest action more intense than any poem. Though he is in pain and his sight is failing as a result of starvation, his spirits are high because hidden in his shirt he has an inspiring letter from a friend:

> they could not know my heart was reading
>   'Courage';
> they could not know my skin was touching
>   'Struggle'.

Such poems usually suggest that the poet has an alternative set of values to those they attack. Of the poets we shall consider in the next section, two — Oku Onuora and Malik — became established as poets on the basis of work written in prison. For both of them, the bitter experience of captivity has sharpened their creative vision.

Poets of street and ghetto

Since the late 1960s an important phenomenon has taken place which has popularised Caribbean poetry on a mass international scale.

We have seen how there has always been a people's language tradition which has been continuous since the very first new song was composed by a captive African. But relatively little was expressed in what we would generally understand as poetry until this recent period. Suddenly, all over the Caribbean there were young poets who were proud to write and perform their spoken language. They were brimful of anger and ideas, and regarded poetry as their best medium of expression. And in London, too, LINTON KWESI JOHNSON was developing a successful fusion of reggae rhythms and the spoken word. Yet, at the beginning, none of these poets from diverse starting points were aware of each other.

The Black Power movement brought about an upsurge of pride in the mass of Caribbean people. In the East Caribbean this was related to the struggle for recognition of the steel band. From Jamaica, it linked with the growing acceptance of the Rastafari movement, which had its own strong *cultural tradition*. Reggae captured a mood, both in rhythms and unforgettable lyrics. Its uniqueness soon attracted international attention. The statements of non-privileged West Indians were at last being recognised.

Dub poetry

The poets whose work is usually linked under this label (Oku Onuora, Michael Smith, Mutabaruka and Linton Kwesi Johnson) were not considered as a group until quite recently. In fact their work is as different as it is similar. What draws them together is that they have all, as **sufferers**, been completely immersed in reggae music, and have lived the experiences the music draws on. Often, and inevitably, their work has echoed reggae rhythms, as here, in OKU ONUORA's *Reflection in Red*:

    an di man
    dem fram Reama
    an Jungle
    a bungle
    a dance
    an a prance
    to some heavy
    reggae ridim

Concrete Jungle and Reama are the two areas of Kingston's Trench Town, which have constantly engaged in political warfare. Against this conflict, Oku Onuora stresses the unity of the communties' response to reggae music.

Many poets who are not personally oppressed have protested on behalf of those who are. The **dub poets**, on the other hand, often maintain that they do not speak with a personal voice, but simply reflect the feelings, experiences and words of the poor. MUTABARUKA has a poem *Call Me No Poet or Nothin Like That*, in which he says the harshness of his situation does not allow him the luxury of crafting his words into 'art'. Oku Onuora speaks

Oku Onuora

as a representative in *A Slum Dweller Declares*:

> yu believe we come ya willinly?
> yu believe wi waan
> wi pickney dem fi grow up
> inna place worse dan hag pen?

The dub poets are well qualified to speak as representatives of the oppressed. None of them began with any advantages.

The **Rastafari** movement has had a profound impact. MICHAEL SMITH celebrated the sense of identity he thus gained in *Roots*, which he always performed to an accompaniment of Rasta drums:

> Jah/jah
> RASTAFARI
> Jah/jah
> Roots are I . . .

Linton Kwesi Johnson

Michael Smith

The style of these poets has also been deeply influenced by the DJs who improvise words to a dub backing track, hence the name, dub poet. Influences include the use of rhymes and games, as we have seen in Michael Smith's work, and strong, direct social commentary. Their closeness to the popular cultural styles gave the poets potential for commercial success. All the poets had been working closely with musicians, but it was LINTON KWESI JOHNSON in London who had the first breakthrough with a successful record: *Dread Beat and Blood*, released in 1978, which spoke of the different but related struggles of the black community in Britain, and the explosive combination of consolation and violence to be found in a reggae dance:

> music breaking out, bleeding out, thumping out fire: burning

The commercial success of the dub poets is to be welcomed, because it has given poetry a popularity and centrality which it has not enjoyed anywhere in the Western world for centuries.

Poets of the panyard

Calypso was there before reggae, and continues to be the first music of the East Caribbean. The 'grooming' of Trinidad's world-famous **Carnival** as a tourist attraction cannot altogether hide the fact that calypso and steelband are just as deeply associated with resistance as dub music is. During the 1930s, **calypso tents** were constantly subject to police raids. Although the censors used the excuse of obscenity, as Atilla the Hun complained in a calypso of the period, they were probably more concerned that calypsonians were most influential political commentators.

Outside Trinidad, Tobago and Grenada, the steel band is often associated with tourist hotels. But in the home of the steel band itself, the **panyard** — where the pans are made, and the bands practise for months before Carnival — forms the focus of grassroots culture.

Poetry has emerged from this musical and cultural environment too. From about 1969, calypso, reflecting more **dread** times, returned to the minor key popular in the 1930s and a less hectic beat. Calypsonians Black Stalin and Valentino performed together with emergent poets like Lasana Kwesi, Chetswayo Murai, Leroy Calliste and Abdul Malik. More recently, a collective known as the 'Network Riddim Band' has developed a style known as **rapso**, which draws heavily on the older poets' work in combination with a Black American disco 'rap'.

Pan is far more than a tourist attraction in Trinidad. It is the life blood of Laventille and other poorer urban districts.

Without relinquishing his roots, ABDUL MALIK has developed his craft as a poet more consistently than others. His work has a dimension rarely expressed in West Indian poetry; that is, his experience as an industrial worker. Here, as in much of his poetry, he seeks to arouse anger and indignation through a reminder of history. In this extract, he captures two opposing *tones*; the commanding voice of power, and the reply of endurance:

> CLOCK AND MOVE MAN!
> CLOCK AND MOVE!
> is centuries now
> I in hey!
> slaverin an
> labarin since
> marnin since
> marnin

'Slaverin' suggests more than one thing. It is an example of a poetic use of double meaning. Can you say how? Rhythms in the poem reflect the monotonous grind of factory work, which through *allusion* is related to centuries of slave labour. What conclusions do you think he wants us to draw?

Do you know what 'Clock and move' means? It is part of the experience of the industrial worker, which Malik brings to West Indian poetry.

Exercises

1. Make a collection of traditional songs which make sad or bitter statements about life.
2. Read Derek Walcott's *Laventille*. Draw the kind of landscape you imagine. Include people within it, still reflecting the mood of the poem.
3. List other possible themes of protest which this chapter does not mention. Can you find poems to fit all of them?
4. Find a piece of **dub** music (the 'B' side of almost any reggae disc). Compose or choose a poem which has injustice as its theme. Practise them together, and then give a performance. (Girls, make sure you get a go.)
5. Topics for essay or discussion
    a) 'The relationship between protest and style in Caribbean poetry.'
    b) 'The influence of reggae music and the Rastafari movement.'
    c) 'Can poetry influence opinion?'

7 Roots and other Routes

As Miss Lou says, in her poem, *Jamaica Oman*:

> Some rooted more dan some

What does **rooted** actually mean? It is an expression used quite a lot, isn't it? It is certainly something to do with being part of the experiences and feelings of 'mostfolks'. It means having a special awareness of the culture and tradition of the people, whose names usually get forgotten in history. And for an artist, it is about turning that experience and awareness powerfully into words, music, dance, etc. Bob Marley was a great roots artist because so many people felt their experience and feelings represented in his music. It is a quality whose value has little to do with schooling and less with money; a quality many of the best Caribbean artists have, and others struggle to find.

Often poets experience the feeling of being apart from the main society. Some through their education and class form part of an elite. There is also a traditional view of a poet as a person apart who expresses individual, personal feelings; often very deep or complex ones which cannot be shared by everybody.

In the Caribbean there has been a hot debate about the role which art and culture should play in life. Many people felt that writers should play an active part in their society, using their writing skills to criticise, to agitate, or offer dreams and ideas to aspire to. Others argued that it was the poet's right to reflect in solitude, with no obligation to be socially 'relevant', and that better poetry was produced that way, anyway. These two different approaches are usually called 'public' and 'private' poetry.

While these distinctions are rather artificial — relatively few poems could be called completely 'public' or 'private' — the argument has followed a challenging period of meeting between poets of very different backgrounds and different views of poetry. After independence, the search for an identity with strong foundations became even more intense. A vibrant culture existed in the ghettoes of Kingston (around the Rastafari movement) and of Port of Spain (around the steelband), as we saw in Chapter 6. The emergence of this **roots culture**, and the poet's troubled search for identity led to a convergence that was to prove extremely good for Caribbean poetry. Roots artists challenged and inspired the 'private poets'. And in turn some began to read and to reflect much more deeply on the possibilities within different kinds of poetry. It was a very important time for learning and exchanging ideas and experience.

Mystical Revelation of Rastafari, the legendary roots band whose sound and message attracted artists, poets and musicians from every section of Jamaican society.

MERVYN MORRIS, in *Literary Evening, Jamaica*, recreates the atmosphere of an event where extreme opposites in cultural approach were coming together. A small group of 'culture fans' have come to hear some poetry from England, which turns out to be full of 'fearfulness and bland negation'. But the major part of the programme is poetry 'by the locals, undergraduates'.

> screaming hot curses, anti-slavery

Although Mervyn Morris is a university lecturer in English, he says he identifies much more with the local 'noisy poems' than the cautious offerings from England. He sees a unity between himself and all the other poets as part of

> a naked nation
> Bracing ourselves for blows

All Jamaicans, he is saying here, are vulnerable in relation to more powerful countries, and it is reasonable to share a common sense of anger.

On the whole, Morris suggests that he is rather detached and sceptical in his poems. *Family Pictures* presents a man apart, whose view of his family is without the rosy glow of sentimentality. The family consists of 'the frazzled wife', 'the bigger boy', and the baby, who chuckles only because

> . . . daddy-man is handy
> to be stared at, clawed at,
> spitted-up upon

He also writes about not wanting to take sides in the public battles that rage around him. His poems revolve around his home and a generally quiet life. It is perhaps surprising that the same man would express such force and anger as he does here:

> I am the man that file the knife
> I am the man that make the bomb
> I am the man that grab the gun
> Study me now

We know that he is not writing from his own experience, but it is an experience with which he can identify. The force and the simplicity reflect those 'noisy poems' for which he stated his sympathy. In fact, Mervyn Morris has had a close association with roots artists. Along with Barbara Gloudon (a journalist) and poets Edward Brathwaite and Dennis Scott, he helped to bring the dub poets to a wider audience, and also to get their work published. Such contacts have positively influenced the development of all the poets involved.

DENNIS SCOTT is another Jamaican poet who writes mostly private, personal poetry which often revolves around family life. A love poem to his wife is entitled *: for Joy*. He portrays himself as a kite which has now swung free and can fly high because of his attachment to her

> So, constant, twine me
> home through waste, through wind
> or hold me high —
> I will hang simple as a child's toy

He has at the same time remained open and sensitive to life outside his immediate circle. He is a dramatist too, and has written, produced and performed in many plays. So he has developed the ability to 'enter into' another character. He can imaginatively enter realms of life which are not his own, but with which he shares strong feelings. If he does not share the beliefs of the **balm yard**, he knows enough of the eerie effects of 'Moon shadow burning' to vividly echo a follower's fears

> I fraid for de shape of de winding —
> de road too crooked,
> it making a rope to twine me!

Dennis Scott

In this poem, *Guard-Ring*, Scott is expressing feelings he has in common with the balm yard follower, of dread and uncertainty, and his sympathy with taking all possible precautions. Though a believer in the protective power of Christ, this person is taking no chances:

> I wearing de ring dem tonight
> one gainst hate and de red pepper

> tongue of malice, a snake-eye
> bone-ring to touch
> if I buck up de tempter

Notice the *metaphor*, 'de red pepper/tongue of malice', which is drawn from everyday life; plain but powerful. And the very familiar tone of 'if I buck up de tempter' makes the terrors seem that much closer and more threatening.

One poem of Scott's raised more excitement, especially among fellow writers, than any other: namely *Uncle Time*. This was because, while written in dialect, the poem made a deep and serious statement. For too long, the use of dialect in drama or poetry had been associated in people's minds simply with humour. *Uncle Time* takes all its images from the natural environment and from folk lore. Time itself is *personified* in 'Uncle Time', portrayed as 'a ole, ole man', who is also 'a spider-man', like Anancy, and 'move like mongoose'. The poem shows Time never at rest, although his effect on the landscape may go almost unnoticed

> quiet-like wid 'im sea-win' laughter,
> scraping away de lan' . . .

But his effect on human lives is much more dramatic and always tragic in the end. The poem warns that when Uncle Time plays with 'yu woman'

> watch 'im! By tomorrow
> she dry as cane-fire, bitter as cassava

See again how apt these *similes* are (dry as cane-fire, bitter as cassava), building up for us a picture of the world in which the speaker of the poem belongs. It is not simply through the language that Dennis Scott makes a **rooted** statement. The whole way of seeing things, of turning aspects of life into characters like Uncle Time, and of expressing difficult ideas by comparing them with something else are drawn from a story-telling tradition which is still the possession of ordinary folk.

WAYNE BROWN is a Trinidadian who went to study at Mona, the Jamaican campus of the University of the West Indies, in the mid-1960s. A close friend of Derek Walcott's, his poetry echoes some of Walcott's complex feelings about the Caribbean. While studying in Jamaica, Brown was actively involved in a radical group which brought together individuals from the **ghetto** and the university campus. His poem, *Red Hills*, reflects the spirit of that time, portraying the tense, guarded nature of a prosperous suburb.

> the instamatic transfiguring glare
> of T.V. sunsets, Alsatians.
> Each evening, each streetlamp long,
> fumbling with padlocks, we keep love in

Outside are spectres of another world which threaten the self-imposed confinement of the hills — a figure 'with red eyes' and an 'unmentionable dog' with 'a hole in its head'. Are these simply figments of the imagination or do they have some basis in reality?

Lorna Goodison

LORNA GOODISON spent her early childhood years in West Kingston, (the **ghetto**). Her mother, however, as we learn in her poem *For My Mother*, came from a well-to-do family. Her parents' wedding was a real society event

> Who anywhere had seen a veil fifteen
> chantilly yards long?

However, after the wedding came a downward slide into poverty. The young Goodison family played round the gully bridge which separated West Kingston from the suburbs. Through the mother's determination, the family did move out to 'concrete suburbia', but the bridge remained a powerful memory and image in Lorna Goodison's mind

> The railings on the bridge
> parallel spell equal still
> and what is now curfew zone
> was then just, Home.
> (From *Bridge Views*)

The bridge here represents both a powerful connection with Kingston's turbulent ghetto, and a sense of separation. Now the poet views the area from the outside, as 'curfew zone'. Once she had known it intimately and uncritically as 'Home'. Goodison's own life has been full of strong contrasts. She is not romantic about poverty, but she feels warmly towards the people who have to struggle with it. She praises her mother's achievement:

> she could work miracles, she would make a garment from a square of cloth
> in a span that defied time. Or feed twenty people on a stew made from
> fallen-from-the-head cabbage leaves and a carrot and a cho-cho and a palmful
> of meat.
> (From *For My Mother*)

Goodison has travelled in America, Africa and Europe, and writes about all her experiences. But her early life is the frame through which she looks critically at her widening world.

ANTHONY MCNEILL was born well-to-do, but, like most Caribbean writers, has striven for a rooted identity in his work. Another Jamaican, he was drawn to the Rastafari movement in the 1960s. He sympathised with a movement which rejected ways of life he himself found deeply disturbing.

> Every stance seemed crooked. He had not learned to fall in with the straight queued, capitalistic, for work.
> (From *Saint Ras*)

Anthony McNeill

Saint Ras is the kind of person who often emerges in McNeill's poetry; someone who is bruised by the cruelty and indifference of 'normal' society. Many of McNeill's poems express anguish at the state of the whole world. *Hello Ungod* portrays a world in total disintegration, using the image of a nuclear attack

> Ungod my lungs blacken
> the cities have fallen
> head sieves in the wind

But the poem suggests that it does not need a nuclear attack to make the poet's mind disintegrate.

> the easy prescriptions
> have drilled final holes in my cells

'Easy prescriptions' suggests attempts to create simplistic solutions to human problems, which may have horrific consequences. 'Cells' is being used in a complicated way here. What different associations does the word have for you? Can you now give alternative interpretations of the poet's meaning?

McNeill is an example of a poet who, distressed by the world around him, found common cause with a roots movement, and at the same time expanded his themes to address a wide range of issues, both local and global.

All the poets we have looked at here appreciated and learned from the work of the dub poets. This did not only work one way. The support of Dennis Scott played an important part in getting MICHAEL SMITH a scholarship at drama school. There he was able to develop his performing skills and came into contact with other poets, whose appreciation helped him develop growing confidence in his own style. OKU ONUORA's poems first came to the notice of Jamaica's literary world while he was serving a prison sentence. Barbara Gloudon, Mervyn Morris and others campaigned for his release. Oku's contact with other kinds of poetry, Black American and Caribbean particularly, encouraged him to compose work which was not strictly dub poetry.

The following poem, *Retrospect*, which we quote in full, portrays a scene reduced to bare essentials, rather like some modern paintings you may have seen. Notice it is in standard English (with one small exception), and contains words like 'etched' and 'cloudless', which are far from everyday talk:

> perched on a branch
> of a leafless tree
> etched against
> a cloudless sky
> a johncrow
> waitin
> for the humanscavenger
> to leave

Michael Smith performing in an art gallery. Support from more established poets opened up a wider range of venues for roots artists.

The ugly reality this poem portrays is not diminished by the 'artistic' presentation. The degradation of the 'humanscavenger' is, if anything, emphasised by such a 'civilised' frame. Oku has continued to concentrate on dub poetry, but occasional changes of style draw sharper attention to individual poems and hence their message.

In Trinidad, there was another dramatic convergence of roots culture and 'private poetry'. In 1967 some secondary school graduates who had ambitions as poets, painters, musicians, came together to form the *Pivot* group. They all wanted to see changes in the society. They held poetry readings and discussion forums. Gradually some members became actively involved in politics. They formed the closest links with roots artists who were composing extremely militant poetry, using the dialect in a way previously untried in Trinidadian poetry.

A lot of questions were asked about the way poets used language. Should they not all seek to capture the special qualities of Trinidadian English? It was felt by some that they should reflect popular creative styles.

CHERYL BYRON, one of several women in the group, began working out her material with musicians and performed in calypso tents. She has subsequently become a popular entertainer.

Cheryl Byron, a popular performing artist in Trinidad.

Victor D. Questel and Anson Gonzalez, the two major poets to emerge from the group, were influenced indirectly. The new view of the poet's role was reflected in different social attitudes. In his poem *A Fairy Tale*, ANSON GONZALEZ sympathises with the student who dreams of 'breaking his teacher's bones', not because he condones violence, but because he condemns the schoolmaster's indifference to the real-life problems of his students:

> Life is sickness and no cash or doctor
> What you teach as life is just a fairy tale.

Gonzalez later became less concerned with such themes. He has continued to render great service to Caribbean poetry through his support and encouragement of other poets and the journal, which he publishes himself, *The New Voices*.

VICTOR D. QUESTEL, who tragically died in 1982 at the age of 33, worked harder than any other poet in the group to capture in words and style the 'heartbeat' of Trinidadian cultural life. He was essentially a 'private poet'. He was more concerned with the printed page than with performance. He wanted Caribbean styles to be studied seriously and was developing new approaches to the subject. He used models broadly from Caribbean culture, rather than from other poetry, to analyse Caribbean poems.

In *Down Beat*, many of the words, stresses and rhythms reflect the hectic quality of the calypso

> Head-lines   a sports page
> Hem-lines   a body line
> Glancing, heckling: all the time

Notice how the phrases are balanced, and nearly repeated but not quite. These are some of the qualities which are catchy in a popular song. However, Questel was not concerned simply to reflect the life he saw, or music he heard. He sought also to combine commonplace images to make statements. In the same poem, the subject 'sways'

> to a rhythm rehearsed in bed
> and the down beat in meh
> head

Anson Gonzalez bestowing an award on his friend and fellow poet, Victor Questel.

> And over head the sun strumming along,
> lashing along meh back

The 'down beat in meh head' becomes one with the sun 'over head', suggesting tension, headache. The next musical reference, 'strumming along' would normally suggest something like carelessness. But used in connection with the sun and reinforced by the brief *allusion* to slavery – 'lashing along', it suggests a harsh and cruel brilliance. The poet thus undermines conventional associations of sun and music with happiness. Why do you think he feels the need to do this?

GORDON ROHLEHR, originally from Guyana, contributed to the new approaches being developed, not as a poet, but as a *critic*. In other words, he loved to read and listen to poetry and discuss his responses both with the poets and others. He was deeply impressed by the work of one of the roots poets ABDUL MALIK. He wrote

41

a long appreciation of Malik's epic *Pan Run* poems, which celebrate the history and culture of Port of Spain's ghetto population. Malik in turn began reading other poets after he became established as a poet. His later work loses none of the spirit of his first angry poems, but it is more controlled. He becomes more interested in the effect words will have on the page as well as the impact which they have in performance. In *Black Womb/Movements*, which expresses a profound faith in the Caribbean and its people, he says,

> we are
> not still
>   born
> we move
> we are
> still moving
> on

By separating the words 'still' and 'born', and then placing 'still' and 'moving' together, the poet creates a sense both of stillness and of movement at the same time. This gives the words a sense of mystery, which echoes even in the simple statement 'we are'.

Contacts between poets such as Malik and Questel, Onuora and Morris, helped to expand range and flexibility. 'Private poets' were challenged to examine their own positions, and to explore the whole range of Caribbean language. More relaxed styles, which encouraged honesty, were one result. Sharing knowledge and experience made the vision of 'Caribbean Unity' seem more possible. This generation of poets have probably addressed more *'universal'* issues than the pioneers of the written tradition we looked at in Chapter 3. *Paradoxically*, it is because they are confidently rooted in a Caribbean 'voice' and identity that they feel free to explore the whole range of world issues and human feeling.

Exercises

1. Is there a regular venue for poetry reading or performance in your town or community? It might be the library or a school, a local hall or 'yard theatre'. Try and find out as many details as you can, and attend one or two events. You may even have your own poems to offer if it is quite informal. Find out from someone involved if there is a regular group of poets and, if so, how they got together.
2. Read Dennis Scott's poem *Guard Ring*. Make a picture of the balmyard believer wearing all the protections described in the poem. Show the eeriness of the moonlit road and suggest the bad spirits which the believer fears to meet. What frightening experiences have you had on a dark night? Do tales of duppies, soucouyants and other mysterious forces still hold the same power?
3. Because the words of Bob Marley's songs live on in the hearts of people all over the world, we could say he is one of the most important poets of the Caribbean. Make a collection of Marley lyrics which have the most meaning for you. You could arrange them under headings like 'One Love', 'Babylon', 'Jah', 'Africa' and so on. With illustrations it could make a really nice book to keep, or to give to someone special.
4. Topics for essays or discussion.
   a) Discuss one or all of the following:
   'poetry is best used to express individual thoughts and emotions';
   'poets should concern themselves with social themes, not their personal feelings';
   'it does not matter what the subject of a poem is, so long as it is beautifully expressed'.
   b) What I mean when I say **roots**.

8 Emergent voices

Is there such a thing as a typical West Indian poet? The simple answer must be no. In this short book we have looked at a wide range of styles and attitudes from dub poets to the formal rhymes of 'Leo' and Tom Redcam. We have seen widely differing attitudes about the relevance of the English *literary tradition*. There is no complete agreement about the types of language most appropriate to Caribbean poetry.

However, if you were able to get all the living poets together at any one time, most of them would have two things in common. Almost all would be Afro-Caribbean and male.

Poems about women rarely reflected their inner feelings.

There have been several *anthologies* of Caribbean poetry in which not a single poem by a woman was included, or at best one or two. East Indian poets have been publishing since the 1930s but their work had little impact outside their community if it took on a distinctive style or subject. Some poets have even adopted a non-Indian *pseudonym* to get wider acceptance. Until recently, many poems by women did not put over a distinctly woman's voice. Without people realising it, the viewpoint of the majority of poets came to dominate Caribbean poetry.

Everyone knows how important the Caribbean woman is in keeping things together through the hardest times. Many male poets have put their recognition of this into poems praising the strength and self-sacrifice of women, particularly their own mothers. We have, for example, ERIC ROACH's beautiful and touching poem, *To My Mother*:

> The image of your beauty growing green,
> Your bone's adolescence I could not know,
> Come of your middle years, your July loins
> I found you strong and tough as guava scrub,
> Hoeing the growing, reaping the ripe corn;
> Kneading and thumping the thick dough for bread.

Women are often portrayed in this strong and competent role. Until recently, most poems about women, whether by men or women, concentrated like a painting on an external image, on what they looked like. These images stir deep feelings in the poet and the reader, but they are not the feelings of the woman who is the subjct of the poem. For example, in a poem called *Market Woman*, DAISIE MYRIE pictures womankind in a general sense. These women all have 'swinging hips and steady stride'. She celebrates these 'hand-maids of the soil' for the fertility of their wombs and the fertility they draw out of the earth in the form of market produce.

Women poets have always written about their feelings, but in the Caribbean have been quite shy about making them public. They were given very little encouragement by *editors* either. In the 1920s and '30s women members of the Poetry League of Jamaica probably outnumbered men. Their work was published mainly because of their connections – they all came from 'society'. Their favourite subject was nature, both Caribbean and English. Most of the feelings they express seem borrowed from books.

UNA MARSON was the first West Indian poet to explore the feelings and particular circumstances of the black woman. She was writing in the 1930s and 1940s. A major theme is that a black woman's natural looks were considered ugly, because people had 'Cinema Eyes'. In the cinema, the only permissible image of female beauty was white, preferably with blue eyes and blonde hair. The woman who is the subject of Marson's poem, *Kinky Hair Blues*, protests against her own menfolk, who have been so blinded:

> I like me black face
> And me kinky hair
> But nobody loves dem
> I jes don't tink it's fair

Una Marson

She is also expressing a pride here in her own kind of beauty, which was not to be heard so powerfully again until the phrase 'Black is Beautiful' captured the popular imagination in the 1960s. However, the same woman cannot hold out against social pressure:

> I's gwine press me hair
> And bleach me skin
> What won't a gal do
> Some kind a man to win

Notice here that Una Marson is attempting a fusion between Black American and Jamaican styles. She has been influenced by the *Harlem Renaissance* (see glossary). At this time the most powerful creative forms of black expression were coming from the United States.

Una Marson was an exceptional person in many ways. She went to England in 1932 and was involved in the movements which led to the political independence of former British colonies in Africa and the Caribbean. She was secretary to the League of Coloured Peoples, and for some time to the Emperor Haile Selassie. Later she was to found the Save the Children Fund in Jamaica. She also started and edited the influential BBC programme *Caribbean Voices*, which played a crucial part in the development of Caribbean literature and its international recognition. It was as an exceptional individual that she got her work published, and it was in London, not the Caribbean. Despite her example, women poets were only rarely included in general collections of Caribbean verse, and still the majority of their work is only to be found in magazines such as the ones we looked at in Chapter 3.

LOUISE BENNETT, as we saw in Chapter 4 was another unusually self-confident and determined person. Although she was to make her name as a performer, she was at first most concerned about getting her work into print. With persistence she finally got half a column in the *Sunday Gleaner* newspaper. People loved the humorous dialect portraits of various Jamaican 'characters'. People soon learnt to read them aloud to enjoy them to the full. Sales of the paper went up, which ensured her a continuing contract. For many years this was the main way in which Miss Lou published. Later, books were to appear bringing together her prolific output.

Louise Bennett's characters are not all women but many of the most memorable are. There is, for example, the 'South Parade Peddler', who one minute tries to coax customers by sweetly flattering them:

> Nice boonoonoonoos lady, come,
> Me precious, come dis way

and the next is giving them violent insults as she realises yet again she is not going to make a sale:

> Teck yuh han outa me box!
> Pudung me razor blade!

For all her efforts, she has little success. As she admits, the 'boonoonoonoos' lady who buys a hair pin is 'De bes one fi de day'. Finally forced to flee by the arrival of the police, she keeps calling her wares:

> Hair pin! Hair curler! Run!

Louise Bennett

We laugh at her straightforward hypocrisy; her sweetness, which goes no deeper than a vain hope that the next passerby may make a small purchase, and her more honest abuse when it becomes clear once again they will not. On the other hand, we also appreciate her determination and persistence.

Louise Bennett's poetry is a more successful development of Una Marson's experiments with the **dialect**. Louise Bennett too portrays ordinary black women as loveable when their behaviour is most natural. In this way she is a challenge to her audience's 'cinema eyes'.

No other woman poet has become a 'big name' in the Caribbean, although Vera Bell published two collections in the USA, and Marguerite Wyke had poems included in an anthology of West Indian poetry in 1958. Gloria Escoffery, Judy Miles, Liz Cromwell and Norma Hamilton were among the women who were publishing their work in journals during the 1960s and '70s.

A volume of poetry called *Among the Potatoes* appeared in England in 1967. It was the work of a Trinidadian poet called BARBARA A. JONES who was at the time a science student. It is a substantial and impressive-looking hardback, with illustrations also by the poet. The poems range over all kinds of subjects. Several express a strong black consciousness and explore the racial problems which occur in England. A greater number are devoted to love, mostly unrequited. Barbara Jones wrote poems which are apparently childlike and playful, but have an underlying deep sense of sadness. Rhymes are always used with a rather jokey effect:

> if only we couldn't feel
> if only we were like seals
> all blubber and fat and all such as that
> if only we were like seals
>
> (from *If only*)

The scientist in her concludes that if we couldn't feel or love, we would be like a stack of computer cards

> then what a dull feel that would feel

The word 'dull' means boring, but also suggests

a dull ache. It is not completely clear whether or not Barbara Jones would prefer that 'dull feel'. Sadly, she died prematurely in New York.

In the late 1970s, one or two slight volumes of poetry by women began to appear. This was the beginning of a new development which is most marked in Jamaica. From almost total obscurity, suddenly some of the most confident and accomplished new poets on the scene are women. This is reflected in the *Savacou* anthology of 1979, *New Poets from Jamaica*, where six of the thirteen poets represented are women. This phenomenon also prompted the publication of an anthology, *Jamaica Woman*, exclusively devoted to poetry by women.

Woman road mender, Grenada. 'Some have surpassed the strength of men.' (Lorna Goodison)

The new confidence is reflected in the subject-matter of the poems. The poets are no longer afraid to reveal their deepest feelings and express a strong concern with the condition of womanhood. We sometimes get a different image of women, which seems to speak from within

> Who is that woman?
> she is fragile there is an egg within her
> in her bosom its always flow-time
> (Lorna Goodison, *Whose is that Woman?*)

This woman draws a deep sense of satisfaction and strength from an awareness of her body functions, while at the same time it is her vulnerability that is stressed.

Vulnerability is an important *theme*. Some women's poems show women having little choice or control in their lives. VELMA POLLARD uses the *image* of a fly enticed into a spider's web. The fly is 'dazzled' by the 'acres of green' that she thinks she sees in the intricate weave of the web. So she enters and sleeps. When she finally wakes up, she discovers she 'can't butterfly', while her captor 'perched outside' maintains the view of 'acres of green'

> you can move
> you can fly . . .
> (from *Fly*)

This type of story, which says one thing, but is meant to be interpreted as something else, is called an *allegory*. How would you interpret the meaning of Pollard's poem?

In a poem by GLORIA ESCOFFERY, the 'baby mother' of a young boy killed while 'playing politics' is caught in the midst of her grief by a newspaper photographer

> . . . forever she throws up her arms
> In the traditional gesture of prayer
> Wai oh! Aie! Eheu! mourns the camera
>   shot matron
>
> (from *No Man's Land*)

'Captured' in photography, the young mother reflects exactly the traditional gestures of woman's grief portrayed in religious paintings. By linking the two, the poet suggests that such tragedy and helplessness is an age-old condition. She asks why this should be so. Why do you think this should be the case?

In a very different way, the suburban housewife in a poem by PAM MORDECAI has very little control over her life. Her routine is trivial, meaningless and repetitive. The phrase 'On Wednesday I fed the children/and dogs' is repeated five times. There is no sense of progress, because the day is always the same. Her environment is making her ill, and seems to reflect her state of mind

> . . . In the sink the dishes
> teetered. My hands were hot
> (from *Wednesday Chronicle*)

Although an ideal for many, this kind of life of a housewife is only 'enjoyed' by a minority. Most women find paid work if they can, which invariably takes its physical toll:

> Some thicken palms with cutlass and hoe
> Split fingers with suds
> Slash nails with fish-knife
> (BRIDGET JONES, *Study fe Teacher*)

The teacher is not left unscathed either. Blackboard chalk gradually 'Stuns the heart/And slowly clogs the lungs' (from the same poem). What do you think the poet means by saying the teacher's work 'Stuns the heart'?

For some women, work means exploiting their bodies. In a poem by CLAUDETTE RICHARDSON, the first woman **dub poet**, a 'go go girl' brings out different responses in her audience. While the men are 'wrapped/in mentally and emotionally' or 'ready to bolt'

> Some women wrench
> Others laugh at what seems a joke
> (from *Go Go Girl*)

The poet concludes that this female spectacle, existing for no purpose besides titillation, does no women any good, however they respond

> Women do you realize
> The joke is all on you

It is not only go go dancers who are used in this way. LORNA GOODISON points out the hidden fate of many domestic servants. Addressing a 'judge man' who 'does not support women's liberation' she retorts:

> They are used to biting their lips under the violation of your sons
> for whose first experience you chose a young clean maid
> (from *Judges*)

Although recognising that she is more privileged than domestic workers, she says she shares one thing in common. Like them she is a woman struggling independently for a living

> They support themselves like me
> Some have surpassed the strength of men

In this poem, Goodison is addressing men who say they want more equality and justice but who refuse to recognise that they themselves may be making women's lives more difficult than they need be.

It is often assumed that when a writer speaks up for women she is attacking men. This is hardly ever the case in the Caribbean. However, most Caribbean women seem to regard romantic love poetry as an irrelevant luxury. They are realists. They express a deep-felt desire for loving relationships with men. There is however a wry recognition that the wider society often overrides the intentions of the individual:

> I wanna hold you
> To console you
> let me cajole you
> and extol you
> Never to control you . . .
> Just can't wait
> till the day
> they parole you . . .
> (PAM HICKLING, *Love Song*)

Lorna Goodison is an artist as well as a poet. This is her sketch of Mother White.

47

Until the 1970s there had been little public sign of a self-confident East Indian voice emerging in Caribbean poetry. Perhaps publishers are reluctant to accept work which is different from their usual expectations of Caribbean verse. Some poets have published privately, which means they have to take on all the costs of producing the book themselves, and all the responsibility for getting it sold. This is often the only course open to Caribbean poets, even those who don't have the problem of breaking new ground. *Savacou* in Jamaica and *New Voices* in Trinidad were both set up by poets simply because there were no other opportunities for getting local work published.

However, an *anthology* of East Indian verse was published in Guyana in 1934. *The Weeding Gang* is one of the poems by its editor, C.E.J. RAMCHANTAR-LALLA. The poem has a very bouncy beat, which partly imitates English poetry rhythms, and partly reflects the Indian percussion instruments which the weeding gang's tools imitate.

> I hear their saucepans jingling
> And their cutlasses a-tingling
> which as their music instruments they play.

The poem uses two Indian words — kheesaz (stories) and boojhowals (riddles). Through these means the poem does create quite a distinctive cultural setting.

One East Indian poet who did decide to publish privately was SELWYN BHAJAN from Trinidad. He has produced a very small volume called *Season of Song*. Interestingly it is printed by the same people who produced Barbara Jones' book. There is a strong sense of 'the beyond' in Bhajan's work, as with other East Indian poets, but in this poem he is simply engaged with a scene of everyday life. A girl is weeding her father's garden. Her simplicity and naturalness are emphasised. Nature, rather than any artificial 'aids', adorns her according to the Indian patterns of female beauty:

> The sun melting at her sides
> Dripped to slip
> Its warmth
> To the green
> Bracelets of grass
> Ankling her bare feet

Another East Indian poet from Trinidad, JAGDIP MARAJ, came to the notice of other poets, including Derek Walcott, through his collection *The Flaming Circle*. The *title poem* tells us that 'the flaming circle' is the route by which we pass to 'that other world of being' (heaven). There is in this a longing to return to the ancestral home, 'to walk among the trees of India' but even more for spiritual enlightenment and peace. The poet is inspired by love — he first glimpsed the flaming circle 'in the heart/of my mother'. At the conclusion, he uses distinctly Oriental imagery to convey his image of heaven. Beyond the heat and intensity of the flaming circle, there is 'the sound of petal on petal'. In other words there would be almost soundless sound, a sound only perceived by concentrating the imagination. There is also the peace of love and security in 'the warmth of hands within my reach'.

In Guyana, several poets of Indian descent have been preoccupied in a very positive way with current issues in their own Caribbean situation. They have not expressed any sentimental attachment to their ancestry. However, an important anthology — *A Treasury of Guyanese Poetry* — was put together by A.J. SEYMOUR in 1980. As well as covering a time span of over a hundred years, East Indian poets are well-represented and amongst their work are some of the most exciting poems.

SHANA YARDAN's poetry reflects an important development. Although of mixed heritage, she often writes about her Indian ancestors. Her most well-known poem is called *Earth is Brown*. The poem is a lament for the death of a grandfather, which for the poet symbolises the passing away of Indian culture in the Caribbean. This culture is associated in a positive and rooted way with the Caribbean through agriculture. There is a continuity between patterns of farming in the 'old world' and the 'new':

> you cannot cease
> this communion with the smell
> of cow-dung at fore-day morning,
> or the rustling wail

of yellow-green rice
or the security of
mud between your toes
or the sensual pouring
of paddy through your fingers

The grandfather's resting place is amongst the cane, where Caribbeans of both African and Indian descent have toiled and suffered.

'Bitter cane' – the heritage of Caribbeans of both African and Indian descent.

A feeling of 'empty placelessness' mentioned by the poet is not in any sense unique to East Indians. It is equally shared by many Rastafarians, or any who yearn to migrate overseas. However, a sense that times have changed gives 'placelessness' a special significance to the East Indian; 'your straight hair (is become) a curse' says the poet. The grandfather's sons have 'city faces'. They have relinquished the security of the soil and must now rely on a 'weekly paypacket/purchasing identity in Tiger Bay'. Yardan suggests that in 'today's unreality' only money can win acceptance. The poet, who more clearly recognises her grandfather's worth, is possibly an indication of firmer new values, however.

The poem is important not only because of the viewpoint it expresses but also because of the special elements of beauty it draws from the Indian tradition into the English language. The whole poem has a *formal* style about it, which suggests it is based on an Indian tradition. The repeated lines

Oh grandfather, my grandfather
you dhoti is become a shroud

give us a sense of a formal *lament*, through which grief is expressed at funerals. The dhoti is a loin cloth. Other elements of Indian culture are associated with a familiar Caribbean setting (the canefield) to create new images

... outside your logie
the fluttering cane
flaps like a plaintive tabla
in the wind

A Hindu temple in Trinidad. Indian cultures have distinctive ideas of beauty, both spiritual and physical.

The logie is a hut, the tabla a high-pitched and very beautiful drum. Just as the tassa drums of Hosay (a Hindu ceremony) are now part of the musical experience of Trinidad, so *imagery* drawn from India can equally become part of the full Caribbean experience in poetry.

Exercises

1. Read *To My Mother* by Eric Roach and *For My Mother* by Lorna Goodison. Compare and contrast the way the poets write about their subject. Can you write a poem about your mother or sister?
2. In the poem *Barriat*, Wordsworth McAndrew of Guyana describes a Hindu wedding as an outside observer. He finds it beautiful and fascinating. He tries to, but does not, understand. He is respectful, but critical. In your class, try comparing 'insider' and 'outsider' views of Hindu and Muslim ceremonies, and of Indian films and music. What do you find the most people are interested in?
3. Look through the Caribbean poetry collections in your school. Can you estimate the percentage of poems by women? Pick out any women's poems you like and start a collection. What do you find are the most common *themes*?
4. Topics for essays and discussion.
   a) 'The contribution of India to Caribbean culture.'
   b) 'What makes the woman's viewpoint different (using poems as examples).'
   c) 'Nobody ever gives me the chance, but what *I* would like to say is . . .'

9 Why is poetry important?

It gives pleasure

Every year sees a high level of cultural activity in Jamaica. Village festivals include street dancing and other celebrations, and also a competitive element, which is part of the national Jamaica Festival. Local winners take part in the finals in Kingston, which always coincide with the anniversary of independence. And just about the most popular section of all is the one where poetry is performed. This has come about since the wider acceptance of the **dialect** poetry of Miss Lou and others, and the encouragement of young **roots** poets like Oku Onuora and Michael Smith. VALERIE BLOOM, who has subsequently published and become a popular performer in Britain, gained her early experience as an extremely popular participant in the Jamaica Festival. It gives audiences immense pleasure to hear their Caribbean language being used powerfully or wittily on stage. It is attractive for performers too because it does not involve expensive equipment or specialist skills, as is the case with music. Nothing is needed beyond the occasional bit of costume or props. The performer needs only to draw on personal experiences and the language which belongs to everyone. On top of that, the performer aiming at excellence requires talent, personality and practice.

It is not only in Jamaica that people have been enjoying poetry so enthusiastically. Members of the energetic Guyanese group including KEN CORSBIE, HENRY MUTTOO, JOHN AGARD and MARC MATTHEWS have performed variously as He-One, Dem Two, and All Ah We, delighting audiences all over the region. They perform the poems of others as well as their own. They have played an important part in increasing awareness of the exciting material being produced in the different countries. Humour and tragedy are bonded together with music and stories, in which the audience is encouraged to participate. It is a full and very satisfying kind of entertainment.

A performance like this can create its own special social setting. The audience is an essential part of what is going on. The poetry itself demands more attention than most popular music because there is less repetition and many more words to absorb. The poetry can provide humour, but also other very intense emotions, as we see in the case of the dub poets.

Many poets are quiet, and not necessarily good performers. In some cases, the printed page may give more pleasure than a performance. When a poem is deep and complicated the meaning cannot always be grasped immediately. Some people find pleasure reading in peace and isolation, as this gives an opportunity for quiet reflection. Most of us enjoy time to think for ourselves.

A contestant in the performing poetry section of the Jamaica Festival.

All of us like some time on our own to think.

It can be powerful

Language is one of the most marvellous possessions of human beings. Think how frustrating babies' lives must be before they can talk, and how much easier it is once they can express themselves with words.

Once we can name and describe a thing, it becomes easier for us to understand it. This is why, at one time or another, all societies have believed that words are associated with magic. Being able to use words gives us a certain power over our surroundings.

We have used both imagination and reason to help us understand the world. Poetic imagination has often helped us to explore our feelings, and therefore to understand them better. Do you think it is more important to understand nuclear fission than human feelings? Which do you think is more complicated?

A gifted poet has a high awareness of language, and can use it to its greatest effect. The poet may not have the instant impact of a rousing political speech, but poetry which is felt to embody truth expressed in a striking way may be remembered and affect people through ages.

It expresses cultural unity

Many people will enjoy the performance of 'a **dialect**' but say they do not like poetry. A complete separation is made between dialect and other really popular poetry on the one hand, and what is considered 'proper' poetry on the other. One problem with making such a firm division is that people miss out on poetry they might enjoy. Another is that even the poetry which is widely heard is not always appreciated for all its seriousness, as happens sometimes when audiences hearing **dub poetry** give the standard response to 'a dialect' — they laugh.

But this 'split' view of the culture, based on the old colonial heritage, is being challenged. Creative ideas can never be imposed from outside, they must grow from within. Out of necessity poets and artists have been asserting and developing the Caribbean viewpoint. This has meant a high level of unity amongst artists of all kinds. The Caribbean is a lively cultural environment where there is free sharing of ideas between musicians, painters and writers, between **ghetto** artists and university lecturers. An increasingly **rooted** poetry of high artistic standards has been one exciting product.

John Agard, a member of the 'All Ah We' team which has done so much to spread enjoyment of poetry in the Caribbean.

An audience of critics

Just imagine you find yourself in a wide open space. You know there are other people about, and you want to make contact. You keep calling out, but you get no response, except a hollow echo. How would you feel?

Sometimes poets feel like that. Poetry is supposed to be a form of communication, but sometimes there is very little response. Poets need critical audiences and readers who will encourage them to strive. Calypsonians have always had to face that demanding test, and have often been rejected but seldom ignored.

A calypsonian faces an audience of *critics*. It is important that students of poetry see themselves as critics, who have a part to play in the process. Being critical is not the same as being negative or destructive. It means that you apply judgement, and are as able to respect the work, skill and perception of a poet as you are to pick out their faults.

A growing number of Caribbean critics of poetry will also strengthen its roots, as you (the critic) apply Caribbean standards of judgement first, and only accept the view of the outsider in so far as it is useful and relevant. This goes for the writer of this book, who is not from the Caribbean. So why not begin your practice of criticism here?

1. Have you any general criticisms of this book?
2. Has the writer left any important areas out?
3. What are the important points on which you a) agree and b) disagree?
4. How do you rate the book in terms of a) balance and b) style?
5. Has it increased your interest in poetry?

Glossary

allegory — a poem, play or picture where the characters and events have a surface meaning, and also stand for a much deeper meaning on another level

allusion — a brief reference, usually only a few words, which makes the reader or audience think of another experience, meaning or work of literature

anthology — a collection of poems or short stories by different authors

autobiography — a personally-written account of one's life

bajan — Barbadian

balmyard — a Jamaican centre of worship and healing which follows traditions derived from Africa combined with Christian beliefs

Robbie Burns — national poet of Scotland who wrote with great feeling for the people and the countryside in the Scottish dialect

calypso tents — at one time real tents, now cinemas and halls where a number of calypsonians play

convention — a feature (of poetry, for example) which is used time and time again by different artists until it becomes a model to follow, a fashion or a habit

creole — an alternative term for **dialect** and generally felt to be more positive. The word **creole** emphasises the mixture of cultures, mainly African and European, which have contributed to the distinctive language of the Caribbean.

critic — someone who carefully studies literature (or art, music, dance, films, etc.) and comments upon it

cultural tradition — see under *tradition*

dialect — used in this book in its special Caribbean sense, this is the word most commonly used to describe distinctive Caribbean speech styles. Miss Lou defines it 'as a manner of speaking, unhampered by the rules of (standard English) grammar, a free expression'. There is a problem with this word, however, in that *standard English* is usually considered a 'proper' language and any West Indian speech style a 'mere dialect' of it. In fact, both are dialects and both are proper languages. One may be more appropriate or expressive than the other in particular circumstances, that is all. It is an advantage to have a wide range of language to choose from. This range is now fully enjoyed by all Caribbean writers. (See also **nation language**.)

dub — basically, the 'drum and bass' track of a reggae number on to which additional rhythms

		literary tradition	see under *tradition*
	and sometimes pieces of melody are 'dubbed in'. DJs like YELLOWMAN perform to the rhythm of dub.	*lyric*	the words of a song or a poem which has the form of a song. Out of this first meaning, lyric has also come to mean a particular kind of poem which is often short, pleasing to the ear, and expressive of an intense emotion or moment
dub poet	a term used to describe some poets whose work is strongly influenced by the rhythms and themes of reggae music, and who often perform their work to a reggae accompaniment		
editor	someone who is in charge of selecting material for book companies to print and *publish*. A person who corrects and prepares any written material for printing.	*metaphor*	when an idea is difficult to grasp we often relate it to something comparable, but easier to understand. When we use one idea as a substitute for another in order to make a difficult idea more vivid in our imagination, we are using a *metaphor*
formal	conforming to official rules; conducted with a sense of proper behaviour		
ghetto	any poor urban area, a major source of roots culture	**Midnight Robber**	a traditional Carnival character who is enjoyed and feared for his elaborate tales of heartless exploits
Harlem Renaissance	a black American cultural movement of the 1920s, which concentrated on black issues with a new sense of pride		
		narrative poem	one which tells a story
		nation language	a term originated by Edward Kamau Brathwaite but now widely used to mean the distinctive language of the Caribbean. It is an alternative to **dialect** and **creole**. It is preferred by many because it implies a united Caribbean nationhood which has its **roots** in what is most independent from the imposed European 'ideal'
heritage	what has been handed down from the past		
image	a mental picture or series of associations set off by words in a poem or in a composition		
imagery	a set of images		
interpret	to work out or explain the meaning of		
irony	a subtle and mild form of sarcasm; can suggest slight self-mockery		
		Negro Spiritual	type of song created originally by black slaves in the United States which is deeply religious and often has freedom or escape as its theme
lament	a poem or song expressing grief over a death		
literal	what words convey on a completely straightforward level		
		oral tradition	see under *tradition*
literature	the collective term for the poems, stories, plays, etc. of any group or culture	**panyard**	a yard which is a permanent practice centre for steel band musicians

paradox	an idea which seems back-to-front but is nevertheless true		popular in the French- and Spanish-speaking Caribbean islands
pastoral	a work of literature in which country life is idealised in a very conventional way	*simile*	a comparison which says that one thing is like another
patois	non-standard French, such as that spoken by the people of St Lucia, who have mostly African **roots**. (Also used in some English-speaking islands as an alternative to **dialect**)	*sonnet*	a European poetry form which was extremely popular until 50 years ago, and is still taken up as a challenge by poets who want to experience writing within very strict limits. Claude McKay and Derek Walcott are two Caribbean examples. A sonnet always has fourteen lines and five 'short-long' beats to a line
personification	talking about things, creatures or ideas as if they were human beings		
phrase	a group of words forming part of a sentence		
Poet Laureate	in colonial Jamaica the highest title of honour awarded to a poet, held by one person only at any time	*standard English*	the English which is officially deemed correct and transmitted through schools, the courts, radio and newspapers, etc.
protest tradition	see under *tradition*		
proverb	a short, memorable saying expressing a fact of everyday experience	*symbol*	something that stands for or represents something else
pseudonym	a false name	*theme*	an idea which is developed through any written work or discussion
publish	to produce and distribute books and other printed material	*title phrase*	a phrase which is contained within a poem but also used as its title
rhyme	occurs whenever two or more words are used whose endings sound exactly the same	*title poem*	a poem included in a collection, whose name is used as title for the whole
rhythm	a pattern of recurrent stresses or sounds	*tone*	signals given out in any piece of language which suggest mood or purpose
Romantic	part of a late 18th and early 19th century European artistic movement, which reacted against rigidity and materialism, and encouraged free expression of the emotions	*tradition*	a set of ideas or way of doing things, which is handed on, drawn from, imitated and adapted. The kinds of *tradition* referred to in this book are:
roots	1. origins; 2. faithful to origins or ancestors; 3. coming from, or expressing the voice of, the ordinary majority of Caribbean people	*cultural tradition*	any established artistic activity, which has its roots in the past
salsa	a dance rhythm especially	*literary* or *written tradition*	stories, poems and other

oral tradition	communications passed on through the printed word stories, poems and other communications passed on by word of mouth		some subjects which are of equal relevance to everyone, everywhere in the world. While this is no doubt true of such things as birth, nourishment, reproduction and death, European writers have often called their views 'universal' because they were unable to appreciate anyone else's
protest tradition	poets who protest against injustice find they share common views and experiences with poets of the past. They draw and seek inspiration from older work, thus contributing to the protest tradition	*verse*	words organised in lines according to our expectations of poetry
'universal'	a very ambitious word, which suggests there are	**yard theatre**	any informal outdoor space where theatre is performed

Further Reading and Listening

Books

Louise Bennett *Selected Poems* ed. Mervyn Morris (Sangster's, 1982). A recent selection of Miss Lou's enormous output, with notes for discussion.

Edward Kamau Brathwaite *Third World Poems* (Longman, 1983). A collection of poems selected from previously published work by the author reflecting his overall view of the world.

Edward Kamau Brathwaite (ed.) *New Poets from Jamaica* (Savacou Publications, 1979). Brings together the work of the dub poets and a number of good, previously little-known, women writers.

Lloyd W. Brown *West Indian Poetry* (Twayne, 1978). The first comprehensive general survey and discussion of poetry in the English-speaking Carribbean.

Stewart Brown (ed.) *Caribbean Poetry Now* (Hodder and Stoughton Ltd, 1984). Many of the modern poems discussed in *Poetry in the Caribbean* can be found in this excellent anthology for schools. It also includes a list of modern Caribbean poets and their works for further reading.

John Figueroa (ed.) *Caribbean Voices* Vol. 1 and Vol. 2 (Evans, 1966 and 1970). An important collection of the earlier established poets' work.

Mervyn Morris (ed.) *Seven Jamaican Poets* (Bolivar Press, 1971). An attractive book, illustrating the best of the more formal modern Jamaican poetry.

Pamela Mordecai and Mervyn Morris (eds.) *Jamaica Woman* (Heinemann, 1980). The only anthology so far devoted entirely to poetry by women.

Andrew Salkey (ed.) *Breaklight* (Hamish Hamilton, 1971). A lively and comprehensive anthology, with an emphasis on social comment and political commitment.

A.J. Seymour (ed.) *A Treasury of Guyanese Poetry* (The Guyana and Trinidad Mutual Fire Insurance Co Ltd, 1980). Brings together the old and the new in Guyanese verse, with emphasis on the new. Indo-Guyanese poets are well represented.

Derek Walcott *Selected Poems* (Heinemann, 1981). Previously published works, selected, annotated and introduced by fellow-poet, Wayne Brown.

Records

A lot of Caribbean poetry can only be fully appreciated when it is heard. Many poets are now 'publishing' on records, as well as in print.

Louise Bennett	*Miss Lou! Yes M'Dear* (Island Records, ILPS 9740, 1983).
Edward Kamau Brathwaite	*Rights of Passage* (Argo, PLP 1110/1, 1969), *Masks* (Argo, PLP 1183, 1972), *Islands* (Argo, PLP 1184/5, 1973).
Linton Kwesi Johnson (Poet and the Roots)	*Dread Beat and Blood* (Virgin Records, FL 1017, 1978).
Paul Keens-Douglas	*Tim Tim* (KeensDee Records, Tim Tim 1-PK-D001, 1975).
Paul Keens-Douglas	*Savanna Ghost: the dialect of Paul Keens-Douglas* (Keensdee Records, Tim Tim 2-PK-D002, 1977).
Abdul Malik	*More Power . . . The Poetry and Music of Malik* (Dam'd Productions, DM 001, 1982).
Marc Matthews, Ken Corsbie, John Agard	*Marc-up: Marc Matthews and Friends* (Theatre Information Exchange, TIE/WO 87, 1978).
Mutabaruka	*Check It!* (Alligator Records, AL 8306-A, 1983).
Oku Onuora	*Pressure Drop* (Blue Moon, BM103, 1985).
Michael Smith	*Mi Cyaan Believe It* (Island Records, ILPS 9717, 1982).

Poets from the West Indies Reading their own Works, ed. John Figueroa (Caedmon Records, TC 1379, 1971). This features Anthony McNeill, Dennis Scott, Mervyn Morris, Derek Walcott, Edward Brathwaite, Frank Collymore, Eric Roach, John Figueroa, H.A. Vaughan.

Also available:

Carribbean Poetry Now

Other books in the series:

Music in the Carribbean
Theatre in the Carribbean
Tourism in the Carribbean
Consumer Affairs in the Carribbean